The
WRINKLIES™
GUIDE TO GROWING OLD
DISGRACEFULLY

First published in Great Britain in 2013 by Prion Books

an imprint of the
Carlton Publishing Group
20 Mortimer Street
London W1T 3JW

A catalogue record for this book is available from the British Library

ISBN 978-1-85375-860-7

Printed in Great Britain by CPI Group (UK) Ltd, Croydon, CR0 4YY

10 9 8 7 6 5 4 3 2

The
WRINKLIES™
GUIDE TO GROWING OLD
DISGRACEFULLY

Mike Haskins
& Clive Whichelow

PRION

Contents

Introduction

To grow old gracefully or to grow old disgracefully, that is the question! Shall we grow old gracefully like a wrinkly old ballet dancer delicately pirouetting into the sunset?

Or shall we grow old disgracefully like a snarling, foul-mouthed, ageing punk rocker stumbling angrily around the stage in an increasing stupor until he finally tumbles off the edge into a pile of old beer crates?

Or perhaps like one of those ladies of a certain age who have extraordinarily coloured hair but who seem to possess no clothes that quite fit them properly and who totter merrily around chortling until they topple off their high-heeled shoes to the ground far below?

Actually, come to think about it, quite a lot of us wrinklies seem to have gone for one or other of these options. We may not have intended it, but that's how we've turned out!

And why not?! At this stage in our lives we wrinklies should be entitled to say, do and dress as we want without worrying what anyone else thinks!

We should feel free to enjoy ourselves in whatever way we see fit! After all these years surely we deserve it! If we want to drink ourselves silly, why shouldn't we? If we want to stuff ourselves till we pop, who's going to stop us? If we want to spend the night pogoing around the dance floor until we drop, let's do it! After all, we might drop sooner rather than later!

And what's the problem with us wrinklies behaving disgracefully? We can spend our days and nights doing whatever we like. After all, if we've retired we don't have to get up for work in the morning like everyone else.

Young people are the ones who should be restricted from excessive drinking and other pleasures in case they cause themselves lasting damage. In contrast, by living as long as we have, we wrinklies have proved ourselves to be born survivors. Now we should be free to indulge ourselves as we see fit.

What harm's it going to do now? Well, possibly quite a lot!

If, however, you've reached wrinklyhood and are still in perfect health, you must clearly have missed out on a number of the world's pleasures during your youth. Later life may then offer an ideal opportunity for a bit of catching up.

And yet people are often intolerant of us wrinklies growing old disgracefully.

They say we're going through a mid-life crisis. Or maybe a three-quarter life crisis. Maybe they think we've gone a bit funny in our old age. What nonsense!

No, we wrinklies can teach the youngsters today a thing or two about being disgraceful and outrageous.

In our time, we were the original rock 'n' rollers, the original teddy boys, the original mods, the original rockers, the original punks and the original duffle coat-wearing, trad jazz enthusiasts.

OK, maybe that last group weren't seen as quite so much of a threat to the social order. Nevertheless people have certain expectations of us wrinklies.

They expect us to be twinkly-eyed and cheery and to have acquired the wisdom of a lifetime of experience. Well, of course we have acquired this. But there's just one problem. We're now having a bit of trouble remembering it all.

People also expect us to behave impeccably like fine, upstanding, venerable senior citizens. Well, we may indeed be venerable, but on the other hand why should we be expected to be fine and upstanding when no-one else is any more?

Why should we have to speak politely when others respond with only an angry foul-mouthed tirade? And the people we meet after leaving our homes are even worse.

Why should we say "please", "thank you" or "good morning" when others seem to think a sneer or a silent gormless stare will serve just as well?

Why should we always have to be neatly dressed when others don't seem to worry what they wear? They go out wearing onesies or dressed as their favourite footballers or dressed as a shapeless mound of well-used polyester or hardly dressed at all.

Why should we have to behave in an exemplary manner when the town centre is filled with young people in an incapable state, fighting and being sick over one another?

The only way we can get down the high street these days is by treating these mounds of degenerate humanity like a series of hurdles.

If these helpless, vomiting youngsters think they're behaving disgracefully, we wrinklies will show them how to do it properly. Not only that, we might manage to have a bit of fun in the process rather than just making ourselves ill and incapable!

So we are faced with two choices. We can grow old gracefully or we can grow old disgracefully. OK, a third option also exists: not to grow old at all!

Unfortunately there are only two ways of achieving this. One is premature death; the other is by having near constant cosmetic surgery on our wrinklier areas.

Clearly neither premature death nor perpetual cosmetic surgery is particularly attractive (in any sense of the word). The former means you will no longer be around. The latter means you will be around, be just about capable of movement (apart from your face), but will look like you have recently had to escape from Madame Tussauds to avoid being melted down.

So never mind that! Come on, grand-daddy-o! Let's grow old disgracefully! After all, getting old is a bit disgraceful in itself! A lot of the effects of ageing would be terrible things to inflict on anybody let alone the elderly.

Let's have some fun while we can! Let's eat, drink and be merry. Or maybe eat, drink and make ourselves unapologetically dyspeptic! Let's get out there and paint the town red. Well, red with a hint of beige, maybe.

Let the wrinkly revels begin!

Unless it's those coffee-flavoured Revels no-one likes!

Chapter 1:
Why Growing Old
Is A Disgrace

How long have you got? Because once you get started, the list might be as long as Twizzle's pyjamas. There you are in contented middle age one minute with the end of your mortgage in sight, the kids off your hands, retirement beckoning with only a slightly wizened finger and all is looking quite rosy. Then...

Creeping up silently in carpet slippers comes old age.

That's the thing about old age: it doesn't suddenly whack you over the head with a walking stick; it shuffles up quietly, sprinkling around whatever is the opposite of fairy dust.

Slowly but surely your 20/20 vision becomes 19/20, then 1820 and so on until eventually it's back in the Stone Age.

Your once pin-sharp hearing loses its top end bit by bit and the first you know about it is when you no longer hear the microwave ping and forget that you were warming up some milk for cocoa.

And talking of forgetting – that's the other thing that is rather disgraceful about getting older.

What were we talking about? Ah yes, the other thing that is rather disgraceful about getting older is forgetting. Forgetting what? Well, pretty much anything of any importance.

Yes, for some reason, the entire lyrics of "Chirpy Chirpy Cheep Cheep" have been lodged in your head forever, but you'll be damned if you can remember your bank pin or all the names of your grandchildren or where the hell you left your specs. Then there's the rest of your body. They say the body is the most fantastic machine in the world. Did you know that in the time it takes you to read this sentence

50 million of your cells will have died and been replaced?

Amazing! But replaced with what? You'd think that if your body was that smart, it would have replaced them with nice new cells. But no, it replaces them with ones that are a bit worse. How stupid is that?

There should be some sort of cosmic complaints department you could go to. 'Disgusted, of Earth' should be able to request, nay, demand, top-notch, brand spanking new cells, not the slightly dodgy biological cast-offs that are left over when all the best ones have been dished out to teenagers and other unworthies.

But whoever said that any of this was fair? Old age comes to us all – if we're lucky.

You have a choice: either you get older and have all the baggage that comes with that, or you don't get older. And we're not talking about not getting older in a Peter Pan/ Cliff Richard sort of way, we're... but let's not dwell on that.

If you're reading this, you've got older. The trick now is to carry on getting older but do it differently. Whoever thought we'd have pop groups of pensioners? Who thought we'd have septuagenarian sex symbols? Who thought 70 would be the new 50? Growing old is a disgrace only if you let it be.

Your Body Won't Do What It's Told Anymore

Has your body ever done what it's told? Like a disobedient child, it just refuses point blank. Diet? In your dreams. Get fitter? Hah! Too much like hard work. Despite appearances, your body is a spotty adolescent that just won't co-operate. So what can you do about it?

Dieting
Of course, the easiest thing is to not bother trying to diet. If people of your age were meant to be slim, why did they invent expandable waist trousers?

The other method is to fool yourself into thinking you're dieting. Instead of stuffing down large chocolates, switch to after dinner mints. They're reassuringly thin. The fact that you can still gorge through half a pound of them at one sitting is neither here nor there.

Exercise
They always say that any work you enjoy doesn't feel like work. So, instead of punishing yourself at the gym three times a week, take up a sport that you really enjoy, such as throwing crockery at your other half or walking round the streets spying on your neighbours.

And don't forget the power of the mind. Scientists have found that just thinking about doing exercise is almost as good as actually doing it. Therefore it probably follows that watching a football match or a tennis match on TV will get you fitter than watching a panel game. Just by changing your viewing habits, you will be Olympics material in no time!

Sleeping

At a certain age you don't need quite so much sleep. You go to bed at 10.30 and, after several hours of tossing and turning, getting up and making cups of tea, reading a book, or finding out the hard way what terrible dross is on TV at 2.00am, you finally drift off at about 3 o'clock. It's that body of yours again refusing to do what it's told.

So, what's the answer? Go to a rave. Or a party, or a dinner party, or the cinema. It doesn't really matter, because as soon as you've been there a couple of hours your eyelids will start drooping, your yawns will come thick and fast and you will be off in the land of Nod before you can say "insomnia, inschnomnia". Just remember to take your pyjamas with you.

Appearance

Whether you use a good moisturizer or not, there's only so much you can do to keep those wrinkles at bay. Otherwise, why would all those famous actors and actresses, who have access to the best make-up money can buy, still have facelifts?

But the answer is to embrace those wrinkles. They're there for a reason. What's the point in being older if you don't look older? Could Alec Guinness have passed as a venerable elder in *Star Wars* if he'd looked like Justin Bieber?

And surely you'd get thrown off buses regularly for trying to use your bus pass if you had fewer lines than the Snowdon mountain railway.

What Exactly Is Ageing?

What is ageing? Well, we all are, aren't we?! But here are a few other definitions to help us understand just what ageing is and why it is such a disgraceful process (especially as there doesn't seem to be anyone to whom you can usefully complain about it)...

• Ageing is just a state of mind – unfortunately your joints, back, feet etc will probably beg to differ.

• Ageing is scientifically defined as being a gradual accumulation of damage. That's a nice way to think of yourself. You're a walking "accumulation of damage"!

• Ageing is the process of things wearing out. This is unfortunate when the thing in question is your body, especially if you didn't keep the receipt.

• Ageing is caused by damage that occurs during everyday life. So if you want to avoid it, sleep during the day and get up at night instead.

• Ageing is a process of physical, psychological and social change. But mainly it involves fewer and fewer people finding you physically attractive.

• Ageing is caused by a build-up of damage in all your cells and organs. So it's probably best to completely replace these every six months or so.

• Ageing is a process that makes it increasingly likely that we will fall ill. So if you want to stay healthy, die young!

Are You Growing Old Gracefully or Disgracefully?

Do the leisure activities you enjoy mark you out as a wrinkly who is growing old gracefully or disgracefully?

Activities enjoyed by normal wrinklies	Activities enjoyed by disgraceful wrinklies
A quiet night in	A very noisy night out
An afternoon tea dance with light refreshment	All-night rave with extremely heavy refreshments
Enjoying a jolly sing song of timeless old classics at home in the evening	Enjoying a jolly sing song of timeless old classics while wandering home at 4 in the morning
Regularly doing a bit of work in your garden	Regularly being found lying unconscious in someone else's garden
A stroll around town	A stroll around town completely naked save for a traffic cone on your head
Visiting local museums and stately homes	Breaking into and raiding local museums and stately homes
Having a good gossip with your old friends	Providing some good gossip for your old friends, if not for everybody who watches the 10 o'clock news
A pleasant drive through the local countryside	Being chased by the police through several counties
A regular visit to the doctor to check everything is still in working order	A regular visit from medical experts interested to find out how you remain in working order

Fings Ain't Wot They Used To Be

Max Bygraves was right, they can't leave anything alone, can they? They've turned the bank into a pub and the pub into flats and everything else into car parks. This is all very confusing for us wrinklies, so here is a guide to establishments old and new.

The fish & chip shop

The quintessential British takeaway is very unlikely to be run by a Brit and now serves up kebabs, dodgy-looking bright pink sausages and all sorts. Even if you find fish and chips being served, it will not be in a newspaper. Elf 'n' safety, no doubt.

The pub

Monday night is "poker night", Tuesday is karaoke, Wednesday is "race night", Thursday is open mic evening, Friday is Quiz night and Saturday is wall-to-wall sport on screens the size of your house. Whatever happened to "popping in for a couple of pints" night?

The supermarket

Whereas once we had off-licences selling booze, greengrocers selling fruit and veg and newsagents selling fags, papers and sweets, we now have supermarkets selling the lot. Some of them even sell petrol, but then petrol stations sell fags, papers, sweets, booze and groceries too. Very confusing!

The bank

Once upon a time bankers were behind bars, and you might think some of them still should be, but that was before the staff started dressing in T-shirts and they were blaring out pop music all day long and you had to serve yourself. Is this progress?

Tattoo parlours
Back in the day, tattoo parlours were slightly dodgy establishments in port towns where sailors could roll up when on shore leave and have "love" and 'hate' stamped on their knuckles. These days tattoo parlours are everywhere – still, something's got to take the place of all those closed-down off-licences, greengrocers, etc.

Nail parlours
Again, you've got to fill up the high street with something, so why not? And what will be next? Hair extension parlours, eyebrow parlours, fake tan parlours? (Oh, they already exist, don't they?)

Charity shops
In the beginning there was Oxfam, now the high street is crammed with charity shops of all descriptions. What was once a permanent jumble sale now sells designer clothes (at designer prices) and has themed window displays – though these shops still always smell a bit funny, don't they?

Pound shops
Even with inflation, they're still "pound shops" though they should probably by now be £1.37 shops or something. Like charity shops, they seem to breed like dole scroungers.

Pawnbrokers
A sign of the times, but at least there are still a few people left with stuff worth pawning. Be worried only when the pawn shops start getting boarded up.

Wrinkly Money: There's No Gold In Them Thar Golden Years

When you're young, you probably imagine a fair amount of your time in old age will be spent counting your vast wealth. After all, a lifetime's work should yield a fair whack of the green stuff, shouldn't it? Oh, the naiveté of youth!

But where's it all gone, and how can you get it back?

Bills

What with the gas, electric, telephone, water and all the rest, it's hardly surprising that you're not exactly rolling in it now, is it? You could try writing to all those providers and claim that you were a victim of identity theft way back when and it's all been a terrible mistake. Well, it's worth a try.

Personal possessions

If you have spent your money on tobacco, alcohol and having a good time, let's hope you haven't wasted the rest. Those youthful passions for trendy clothes, LP records, stamp and coin collections etc may well be the pension plan you never knew you had – if you've kept them. If, though, it's tank tops and Donny Osmond records, you may be in for a disappointment.

Your mortgage

With a bit of luck your mortgage is near, or at, an end. That house you bought for two and sixpence back in the mists of time is now worth as much as Buckingham Palace was then! All you have to do is move out of it and cash in your chips. True, you will be homeless, but oh how rich you'll be!

Food and drink
Well, you can always see where one bit of your earnings went.
Look in the mirror, turn sideways, there it is! Just when it was
too late for us, the government invented the idea of healthy
eating and made five portions of fruit and veg a day a legal
requirement. Perhaps if we try and up our current intake to
500 portions a day it will balance out all those days in our
youth when five a day meant some Fruit Pastilles, some Jaffa
Cakes and a few leaves from the tobacco plant (burnt and
taken bronchially as an inhalation).

Fags and booze
Yes, a lot of your money has literally either gone up in smoke
or straight down the toilet. Some wrinklies might remember
a time when smoking and drinking were recognized, if not
as health products, then certainly as the officially recognised
outward signs of being a grown-up. The authorities then
decided to tell us that these pastimes were, in fact, extremely
unhealthy. As we had already foolishly allowed ourselves to
become addicted, the government decided to teach us a lesson
by piling a load of tax onto the offending items. Nevertheless,
some defiant wrinklies have carried on smoking and drinking
themselves into penury and have even risked freezing
themselves to death outside in the cold air when smoking
inside pubs was banned. These brave souls should surely
be given a medal!

Your kids
If you had any cash left over, this is surely where it all went.

The World Is Moving Faster Than You Are

Let's face it, everything is moving faster than you these days. Though has everything really speeded up, or are you just getting slower?

It seems like just yesterday that you were boogieing the night away without a thought about tomorrow. And now it is tomorrow. Yes, time really does fly when you're having fun, doesn't it?

So, how do you put the brakes on a bit? How can you slow the world down to your speed? Here are a few suggestions:

• When everyone else puts the clocks back, leave yours alone and the rest of the world will be, for once, trying to catch up with you. If you do this every year, you will eventually find the world is several hours behind you and completely unable to catch up.

• Fashion is cyclical, so when everyone else is reviving the 80s, say, you go off on a 90s kick. The world will be floundering in your wake.

• The calendar is, frankly, a purely human invention. If you say it's 1966, then it can be, and you've still got the Summer of Love to enjoy.

• Cryogenics. Yes, it's an extreme option, but if you have yourself frozen, and go into storage for a few decades like an unwanted pack of fish fingers languishing at the back of the freezer, you will emerge to find that everyone else has got older. Yes, even One Direction will have wrinkles!

• Some eastern mystics can, by the power of thought alone, slow down their own heartbeats to about one a minute. Your heart normally beats about 72 times a minute, which means that following in the sandalsteps of the yogis, you will live 72 times longer than the average person!

• You remember how boring Sundays used to be? Everything was shut, nothing happened, and the only highlight was the Sunday roast. But it made Sundays seem never-ending, hence the phrase "a month of Sundays". Well, the trick is to live every day like a Sunday. It could be a bit boring, but think how long it will seem!

• One of the reasons the world seems to be moving faster than you is because, er, well, the world is moving faster than you, you old slowcoach! You, therefore, have to get quicker, which is why some older folk get mobility scooters. They don't even need them half the time, they just enjoy whizzing past youngsters and putting the wind up them. Failing that, how about a skateboard?

• Travel faster than the speed of light. OK, that's not going to be easy, especially with your knees, but now that the first commercial space flights are beginning, surely it's only a matter of time before you can board a spaceship, travel in excess of 299,792,458 metres per second, and hey presto, you'll be back before you know it. In fact, if our calculations are correct, you'll be back before you left!

The Seven Signs Of Wrinkly-ness

According to adverts for beauty products called things like Oil Of Wrinkly, there are seven signs of ageing. These are not, however, as you might expect: your hair falls out; your teeth fall out; you fall over; your waist keeps expanding; you move less and less quickly; everything hurts (at least a bit); and all the films, music, and TV shows that you really like were made at least 30 years ago.

But just what are the seven signs of ageing?

Wrinkles & fine lines
Yes, of course we wrinklies have got wrinkles! That's pretty much a given! You could rub over our faces with a piece of tracing paper and produce a detailed road map of the local town centre. There's probably not much we can do about this now. It's either enough collagen injections to try to puff our wrinkles inside out or, for those on a budget, Polyfilla. To be honest, there's little point trying to do this. If you puff all your wrinkles out, your face may end up twice as big as when you started.

Non-uniform skin
What does this mean? Who has uniform skin? When they strip naked, does it look like they have epaulettes? OK, these days our wrinkly skin probably looks a bit more like a patchwork than a uniform. But to give it its due, it's probably covering a slightly larger area than it used to and it still manages to keep everything held in. Just about!

Dryness
Wrinklies can suffer from extremely dry itchy skin and if a wrinkly stands naked in front of an electric fan something akin to a Saharan dust storm may result.

Unequal pigmentation

Just look at us wrinklies with our non-uniform skin and our unequal pigmentation! The people at Oil of Wrinkly seem to be suggesting that we look like something that Baron Frankenstein stitched together in his laboratory using a load of spare parts. We shouldn't worry about unequal pigmentation, though. Not unless people approaching us from the right side think we are a different nationality to those coming from the left.

Lack of luminosity

What are we supposed to do about this? Have a 100-watt light bulb strategically inserted somewhere? Are the people at Oil of Wrinkly worried they won't be able to find us in the dark? If you're concerned that you're not luminous enough, try moving next door to a nuclear power station!

Dark spots

They used to be called liver spots and occur as we get older because of our exposure to ultraviolet radiation from the sun during the six or seven nice days we've enjoyed since our youth. Alternatively they may occur because people keep slapping you with bits of liver.

Visible pores

When we were young, our pores were forever getting clogged up and giving us spots and acne. Now we're a bit older, our pores are great yawning open chasms. Our pores must hate us! What did we ever do to them?!

Wrinklies Growing Old Disgracefully: A Spotter's Guide – The Ladies

Wrinkly Growing Old Disgracefully Type	Distinguishing Characteristics
The Merry Widow	A curvaceous and bubbly lady who is clearly no longer in too great a state of mourning for her late husband but who is still quite merry as a result of drinking regularly to his memory
The Wicked Witch Of The North	A lady with masses of wild and unkempt grey hair who apparently lost her hairbrush some years ago and has spent the time since in a wind tunnel; professes not to care what she looks like; possesses a large number of pet cats who spend a lot more time on personal grooming than she does
The Surgeon's Experiment	Possesses a face unlined and incapable of movement after apparently having received a 3-for-2 offer from the local cosmetic surgery clinic; the immobility of her face makes it very difficult to gauge her reactions, which must have made it difficult for the surgeon to assess if she was happy with the work he had done
21 Again	Instead of dealing with ageing by trying to reverse it, this lady has taken the option of completely ignoring it and dressing as she did when she was a tiny percentage of her current age; causes male observers many surprised looks when she turns round to face them

Wrinklies Growing Old Disgracefully: A Spotter's Guide – The Gents

Type of Wrinkly Growing Old Disgracefully	Distinguishing Characteristics
The Ageing Lothario	A suave but crumbling mix of Peter Stringfellow and Leslie Phillips, who finds slightly saucy innuendo in every single mundane comment anyone ever says in his hearing; perpetually engaged in the now slow-motion pursuit of anything in a skirt as though possessed by the ghost of the sex drive he had in his youth
Elvis Lives	Has a body that is being held together by well-worn motorbike leathers or by his old teddy boy outfit; possesses thinning hair that used to be greased back but which now has to be desperately greased forwards in an attempt to form a quiff from the hairs growing from somewhere down the back of the neck
The Psychedelic Pioneer	Experimented heavily with drugs in his youth and has never quite found his way back to this dimension since
The Overgrown Boy Racer	Can't move quickly on his own, but put him behind the wheel of a car and he's away; spends his time polishing his sporty motor until it glistens like his balding pate

Chapter 2:
Mutton Dressed As Lamb
– Fashion Options For The
Disgraceful Wrinkly

They say that "clothes maketh the man". Well, clothes certainly maketh the disgraceful wrinkly. If there's one thing that announces that you're a wrinkly who's decided to grow old disgracefully, it's the clobber that you've put on to go down to Aldi!

If you see a wrinkly wearing a tight leather mini-skirt, fishnet tights, leather thigh boots and a sparkly boob tube, you know they're going to be the life and soul of the party. Even more so if they turn out to be a gentleman wrinkly.

There are, of course, types of clothes that wrinklies are expected to wear. These are made of polyester and are beige in colour. Many wrinklies opt for this style.

Possibly they are labouring under the misapprehension that there is some sort of official decree which states that those of a certain age must wear beige at all times or they will risk losing their pension.

Why beige? Is it because those of us who are in the autumn of our years are expected to be the same colour as a withering leaf or a decomposing apple?

Or is it some form of camouflage? We wrinklies are being forced to wear beige so we will blend into the background and young people won't be offended by the sight of us!

Either way, it's a disgrace! We, the disgraceful wrinklies, must take a stand and dress as brightly and as colourfully as we like!

Why are only young people allowed to wear tight, bright, colourful clothes? Does some sort of age restriction apply to sales of this attire? Is it a bit like the classification of cinema films? Might you get to a shop counter one day and be told, "I'm sorry, madam, sale of these thongs is restricted to those aged 25 or under."?

Why are we being prevented from wearing the clothes we want? Well, the answer is obvious. Clearly the authorities are concerned that if we dress in youthful clothes, this will mislead others into thinking that we genuinely are young.

So be warned. If someone picks you up in a bar only to then discover in the cold light of day that you are a wrinkly, they may be able to prosecute you under the Trades Descriptions Act.

But why shouldn't we wrinklies dress in tight leather? Our skin has gone a bit leathery these days although admittedly it's not quite as tight as it used to be.

Why shouldn't we dress in bright colours? If we suffer from varicose veins, they will blend in perfectly!

Why shouldn't we show off a bit of flesh? What do you mean, "Look in the mirror!"?

So let's squeeze into our tight tee-shirts, our low-cut blouses, our platform boots, our paisley shirts and our day-glo jackets. People will see straight away that we are wrinklies growing old disgracefully!

Not only that, they'll be able to see this from quite some distance away!

How To Keep Up With The Latest Fashions

This won't be easy because wrinkles are never in fashion, but Zandra Rhodes and Vivienne Westwood aren't exactly spring chickens, are they? Neither are Karl Lagerfeld or Ralph Lauren. In fact, they're a bunch of wrinklies, aren't they?

So for you this means that if you follow fashion you will look ridiculous, but if you create fashion you are allowed to be... shall we say "more mature"?

Simply set yourself up as a fashion designer and you can call the shots.

When men get to a certain age, they don the wrinkly uniform of grey or tan windcheater, grey or puce trousers and a flat cap. The trick is to get this stuff being modelled by youngsters and suddenly it will be cool. In fact, as we write, the humble flat cap is being sported by people such as Brad Pitt, so if you see him any time soon with glasses held together with sticking plaster and a pair of supermarket trainers you'll know things are going in the right direction.

Women of a certain age often find that somehow or other their hair turns blue. This might be OK if you're Marge Simpson, but is it ever going to be trendy?

Well, thanks to Lady Gaga, it is. So, ladies, anything goes. Dresses made of meat, make-up that might have been applied during a power-cut, whatever takes your fancy – though perhaps not sensible shoes and a cardie. Though you never know with Lady Gaga....

Dos and Don'ts On Fashion Accessories For Wrinklies Growing Old Disgracefully

Do: Consider having a tattoo done.
Don't: Try doing this yourself using your old Singer sewing machine which you have wired up to a bottle of Quink ink.

Do: Wear lots of outrageous heavy jewellery.
Don't: Wear so much that the cumulative weight renders you incapable of movement.

Do: Consider covering your face with a large amount of colourful bright make-up.
Don't: End up looking as though someone recently shoved a strawberry trifle into your mush.

Do: Achieve a punk rock look by wrapping lengths of chain around you.
Don't: Find you have inadvertently locked yourself to your bike.

Do: Consider glamorous shoes with high heels.
Don't: Wear heels so high that you risk serious injury if you fall off them.

Do: Look stylish by reviving the fashion trends of your youth.
Don't: Go out looking like you haven't bought any new clothes since 1975.

Do: Create a fashionable look using outrageous combinations of different styles.
Don't: Walk down the high street dressed in nothing but a pair of outrageous combinations.

How To Relive The Fashion Trends Of Your Youth

At your age you could feel a bit self-conscious trolling around in a Kaftan and beads, or Ben Sherman and Crombie, but, with a little bit of ingenuity, those things can be adapted for your age group.

Youth Trend	Wrinklified Youth Trend
Hippy bells dangling from string round neck	Reading glasses dangling from string round neck
Joss sticks	Plug-in air fresheners
"Granny" glasses	Er, granny glasses
Jacket from army surplus shop	Jacket from Salvation Army charity shop
Flowers in hair	Flowers in hairpiece
Skinhead hairstyle	For men, this may not be a matter of choice
Hot pants	Still warm, freshly ironed slacks
Motor scooter	Mobility scooter
Leather jacket	Leathery skin
Trousers with absurdly large flares	Trousers with absurdly large waists
Trousers worn low on hips to look trendy	Trousers worn low on hips to accommodate fat stomach
Black tights to look sexy	Black tights to cover up varicose veins
Facial hair for men	Facial hair for women
Bay City Rollers tartan	Shortbread biscuit tin tartan

Your Individual Takes On Fashion

It's all very well being a dedicated follower of fashion, but if you really want to be cutting edge you have to have your very own signature touches:

The hat
Any fool can wear a baseball cap back to front, but wearing a cloche or a bowler back to front takes real skill to ensure that anyone's going to notice it's on the wrong way round.

The little black dress
Yes, ladies, that staple of any woman's wardrobe. The only problem is that while the dress may have remained little, you may not have done. The trick is to have exactly the same dress in three different sizes so you keep all your options open depending on how the diet is going.

The tie
A lot of men these days (particularly the slippery ones, such as politicians) seem to have ditched the tie altogether. Frankly, that's not good enough. We have standards. Voilà: the see-through tie. This means that, technically, you are still wearing a tie – which might be required for certain formal occasions, but nobody can see it, which brings you up to date. The only drawback is that you might be mistaken for a slippery politician.

The jeans
There's nothing that marks the wrinkly out more than cheap, ill-fitting jeans. Yes, buying your jeans from a supermarket makes sense when you're on a pension, but who said you have to wear jeans? Buy a kilt. There's something about a kilt that is beyond fashion. Not cool, just slightly cold.

Hats For Disgraceful Gentlemen Wrinklies

A jaunty piece of millinery is surely a must for the gentleman wrinkly. But which is most disgraceful?

Trilby at a jaunty angle
Perfect to denote the ageing spiv or Flash Harry type. Who knows what he might have in his suitcase to sell you!

Cowboy hat
Balanced on an ageing wrinkly's head, it says, "I'm cool, rough, tough and perhaps ever so slightly balding."

Little leather cap with metal chin strap
Wearing one of these will quickly attract a whole range of exciting new young male friends.

Panama hat
Officially denotes a wrinkly who likes the odd tipple while sitting out in the sun to watch the cricket.

Beret Denotes an ageing wrinkly intellectual – who again likes a tipple or two… or eight.

Davy Crockett hat
It may make a wrinkly look as though he is King of the Wild Frontier or it may make him look like his wrinkly old cat has gone to sleep perched on the top of his head.

Hats For Disgraceful Lady Wrinklies

Lady wrinklies (or wrinklinas as they are sometimes known) have even greater scope for disgraceful headwear – a fact that anyone who has ever attended a wedding will already know.

Anything large and floppy
Many wrinkly ladies have large and floppy husbands, so why not have a large and floppy hat as well? These are especially useful for wearing to the cinema, theatre or anywhere where they can be used to obscure the vision of hundreds of people sitting behind you. Be careful, though, in case your hat is so large and floppy that it catches the breeze and carries you into the air like an impromptu paraglider.

Bowler hat
On a good day this might give a wrinkly lady a sexy look like Sally Bowles from *Cabaret*. If, however, the effect is more like Laurel and Hardy, the bowler may be best avoided.

The Lady Gaga telephone hat
A hat with an old-fashioned telephone balanced on top of it. Well, it could be handy. Wrinklies are forever forgetting where they left their mobiles.

The Princess Beatrice hat
One of those funny things that looks like a small toilet seat with an ornate surround, as worn by Princess Beatrice to the Royal Wedding. Not only does it look disgraceful, you can try using it to pick up broadcasts on Sky television.

Anything involving large amounts of fruit
The desired effect may be Carmen Miranda, but you may end up looking like something from the gardengrocers.

The Wrinklies' Guide To Getting Things Pierced

If you want to grow old disgracefully, why not consider getting some piercings done? They're all the rage with the young people.

And what's more, because our ears and noses and certain of our other appendages seem to have kept on getting bigger and bigger through our lives, we have lots more space to fit the piercings in. Some wrinklies could probably hang a pair of curtains from their massive earlobes.

Of course, normal piercing guns may prove insufficient to penetrate the thickened flesh of some wrinklies. Instead, some kind of Black and Decker power tool may be required or, in extreme cases, perhaps a hydraulic press from the local dockyard would be best.

Passing through a metal detector may also present problems. Heavily pierced wrinklies who have to remove all their piercings may then be faced with a major reconstruction job to put themselves back together. Some may actually collapse into a heap on the floor when it becomes clear that it was only the piercings that were holding them together at their advanced age.

Young people tend to favour getting their ears, noses or eyebrows pierced. A stud through the eyebrow or nose if carefully situated by a qualified architect could help some of us wrinklies look slightly younger.

A metallic stud can act as a small rivet in an older person's face and will help to hold a mass of wrinkles, bags and jowls from drooping down towards the ground. Don't forget, though, that if the stud is taken out a small avalanche of wrinkly flesh will probably result.

Nipples and other private areas might also have a few metallic objects shoved through them. This, however, would surely be a mistake for any wrinkly. You could run to catch a bus reassured by the loud jingling noise coming from your trousers that you have sufficient change available for your journey. Once aboard, imagine your embarrassment when a rifle through your trousers reminds you that the jingling did not come from a pile of 20 pence pieces in your pocket after all.

Similarly a piercing through the eyebrow may look cool and trendy to some. To an ageing wrinkly, however, it could provide a helpful form of exercise. Instead of lifting weights at the local gym, the pierced wrinkly can exercise just by raising his or her eyebrows a few times. The effort required to lift that small lump of metal in the eyebrow will help an ageing wrinkly burn off several hundred calories.

A stud through the side of the nose is also fashionable, although this should be avoided by wrinklies prone to sinus problems. Blow your nose too hard, and that stud could fly out like a bullet and injure a small child or animal.

Also, if you do start to have a lot of piercings done, remember you may run into problems. A pierced wrinkly could be suddenly swept into the air if they stray too close to anything exerting a strong magnetic field.

How To Spot A Wrinkly Supermodel

Could one of those gorgeous models striding up and down the catwalk with Kate, Gisele, Naomi and Heidi be a disgraceful old wrinkly? Just what are the telltale signs to help you spot a wrinkly supermodel?

• They go up and down the catwalk using a walking frame;

• They've still got their coat and scarf on over the top of whatever outfit they are meant to be modelling;

• They're the only one of the supermodels who has brought a nice piece of cake and some chocolate biscuits to have during their break;

• When they get to the end of the catwalk, they have a nice sit down for a few minutes;

• When they get to the end of the catwalk, they stand there calling for their cat to come in;

• When they pass by up the catwalk, the audience is left with the delicate smell of Vicks Vapour Rub and Werther's Originals;

• They get a bit lost halfway up the catwalk and have to ask for directions;

• They can be heard from the dressing room telling the other supermodels to eat something properly and cover themselves up or they'll catch their death of cold;

• They have a stair-lift installed to get up onto the catwalk.

Nudism As A Clothes Budgeting Option

This is where you can kill two birds with one stone. On the one hand, you are saving piles of cash by not wasting it on such fripperies as jackets, trousers and shoes; on the other hand, it opens up a whole new world that you may never have experienced before.

Naked badminton, for example. Incidentally, why is it that nudists always play badminton? What's wrong with Monopoly? Naked badminton seems to carry with it certain dangers, risks and occasions for embarrassment. (Feel free to put in your own shuttlecock joke here.)

Have you ever added up what you've spent on clothes over the years? Even a modest couple of pairs of shoes a year will set you back about £100 these days.

Over the years you must have spent thousands, perhaps tens of thousands, even hundreds of thousands if you're Imelda Marcos or Elton John.

Now couldn't you have put that to better use? Look at these calculations:

One pair of shoes = 10 bottles of wine

One winter coat = 20 boxes of chocolates

See, you've wasted it haven't you? When you think about it, nudism is a very sensible option. Just one thing, though – if you're going to do it, remember to emigrate somewhere nice and warm first. There is a reason that Britain is not filled from coast to coast with nudist colonies.

Chapter 3:
Inadvisable Sports, Hobbies and Pastimes To Take Up In Later Life

There is probably a very good reason why people take up golf in later life and not, for example, Australian rules football or bullfighting.

You don't often hear of golfers being drugs-tested, do you? Maybe it's because playing golf is barely more strenuous than opening a tin of sardines. In fact, opening a tin of sardines or anything in one of those hard plastic packs – like a new toothbrush, for instance – could burn off far more calories than a bit of gentle golf.

So perhaps that's a good rule of thumb: before you consider taking up any new sport as a wrinkly, first check whether it is a drugs-tested sport. If not, then it's probably safe.

If you ever hear of performance-enhanced Scrabble matches being uncovered by the Sunday newspapers, it's probably time to admit that, ok, fair do's, it's perhaps a bit risky at your time of life.

The same goes for hobbies. Sometimes, as people get on in years, and perhaps after retirement, they find they've got a bit of time on their hands to spend on something enjoyable and interesting, such as researching their family tree.

Well, on the face of it, that sounds pretty harmless. But beware! The shock of finding that one of your nearest and dearest was a mass murderer or a senior figure in the Inland Revenue could prove fatal.

Speed dating could be a no-no too.

In fact, anything with "speed" in the description should set the alarm bells ringing for the average wrinkly.

If you're going to start dating in later life, you don't want all the excitement to be in racing against the clock and giving yourself a coronary before you've even met the wrinkly of your dreams.

When you think about it, there are very few risk-free sports, hobbies and pastimes for the time-rich wrinkly.

Knitting, for example. Any pastime that involves implements with sharp points is fraught with danger. Just by tripping over the cat while taking your knitting to another room could result in a tragic and fatal impalement.

Stamp collecting is riskier than it sounds, too. Licking the back of a postage stamp could mean picking up a deadly virus from the previous owner. Accidentally swallowing said stamp and choking on it could spell cremation curtains for you. "Death by twopenny blue" is a sad epitaph for anybody.

Perhaps the answer is that, if everything is potentially fatal, you might as well go for the most dangerous pursuits imaginable and to hell with the consequences.

Wrestling with alligators, blindfold skiing, arguing with hoodies, trying to form a human pyramid on the back of your mobility scooter... it could all be in a day's play for the wreckless wrinkly. And why not, as Barry Norman may once have said. Go on, you're only old once.

Extreme Sports For The Not So Young

Extreme sports can be pricey, so here are a few ways that you can participate without breaking the bank:

Water-Skiing
Fit a wooden board to the bottom of your Zimmer frame and, hey presto! You have an instant water-skiing device!

Snowboarding
Collect and store your dandruff until you have enough for a serviceable mini-mountain in your back garden. (If bald, athlete's foot powder will suffice). All you need to complete the necessary equipment is an old tea tray.

Wakeboarding
Simply tag on to a funeral procession whilst riding a skateboard.

Bungee-jumping
You always knew that extra-strong knicker elastic in the sewing box would come in handy. Simply attach around the middle of your body and leap from great heights – perhaps your partner's stomach while lying in bed would be a good starting place.

Extreme ironing
This is meant to be simply ironing in unusual places – for many ageing houseworkshy husbands, though, that could mean their own front room.

Kitesurfing

Now that grandchildren sometimes possess kites the size of double-beds with dual hand controls, an ageing grandparent may unwittingly find themselves "enjoying" this sport without intending to, simply by grabbing the controls to "have a go" while standing on a particularly windy beach.

Note: If on a cliff top at the time, said grandparent may also enjoy their first experience of hang-gliding.

Hang-gliding

If the above method doesn't grab you, jump up onto the washing line next time there's a high wind. If that doesn't put you off, nothing will.

Abseiling

A rope attached to the top of the banisters will not only provide you with serviceable cheap and cheerful abseiling equipment, it will also save you a fortune instead of getting a stair-lift when the time comes.

Skydiving

Next time you're on a plane, find the biggest fellow passenger you can find and start an argument with them. You'll be having your first skydiving experience before you know it!

Teapot juggling

This extreme sport hasn't actually been invented yet, but it is surely only a matter of time. Playing "keepy-uppy" with three pots of scalding hot tea is surely extreme enough sport for anyone.

Giving Harmless Hobbies
A New Twist

As soon as you tell someone that you collect stamps or spot train numbers, they make all sorts of assumptions and judgments about what type of person you are.

If you tell someone you enjoy baking or collecting china ornaments, they'll think they know everything there is to know about you.

The thing is then to confound their expectations by giving those old-fashioned hobbies a new twist. For example:

Stamp collecting
Forget postage stamps; collect tramp stamps! Yes, you know those tattoos that a certain sort of woman has on her lower back, which are revealed only when she bends down in the supermarket to grab a tin of beans or tell her toddler to shut up.

Obviously it's going to be tricky trying to get them into an album, but you could make yourself a modern version of one of those I-Spy booklets and get extra points for ones in green ink or misspelled ones, or ones that haven't been hideously stretched by the expanding girth of the wearer.

Train spotting
Simply spotting a train at all on some lines would be worthy of recording, let alone jotting down all the numbers of any that happened by. Yes, train spotting is a challenge, but why not spot something even more rarely sighted? How about policemen, or polite children, or lollipop ladies, or off-licences or greengrocers?

Bird spotting

Is sitting in a field stock-still for two hours in the hope of spotting the speckled doo-dah anyone's idea of fun? There is probably a reason why these birds' names are often pre-fixed with the phrase "lesser-spotted".

Walking around your neighbourhood after dark with a pair of binoculars may result in fewer birds being spotted but could perhaps be more fun – especially when people forget to draw their curtains.

Baking

What could be more genteel than rustling up fairy cakes or fondant fancies before guests arrive? But you can spice things up – quite literally – by adding Tabasco or chilli powder to every third one. The hint of danger when your guests choose their cakes will make your tea parties the talk of the town.

Collecting china ornaments

Collecting these can be delightful, but oh so expensive. And some people regard such a collection as a bit old-fashioned and twee. Save yourself a fortune and earn the gasps of your visitors by proudly displaying on the mantelpiece your collection of bones.

After a Sunday roast and the Monday cold meat sandwiches, you are left with a bone or three that simply gets thrown in the bin. With a little bit of ingenuity and artistic flair, these bones can be transformed into objets d'art with a dash of paint or glitter. Who knows, it could herald the start of a new TV talent show: *Bone Idol*.

Why Getting Down With The Kids Is Not A Good Idea

After a certain age, your body has ways of telling you that it is no longer young and demands being treated with a bit of care and respect.

Fooling around like some young flibbertigibbet will incur the wrath of your ageing chromosomes. In other words, they will make you pay for it.

Activity	Result
"Getting down" to the music at a family gathering	Getting sent down to the local A&E unit
Trying to look cool	Leaving everyone else cold
Trying to look "hot"	Not even getting warm
Wearing earplugs to listen to music	Everyone will think it's a hearing aid
Wearing tight clothes to look cool	You will be cool only in the sense that your blood has stopped circulating
Hanging out in the right places	Hanging out in all the wrong places as your body defies gravity
Adopting teenage slang	Attracting teenage abuse
Buying an expensive motorbike	Having to buy expensive insurance
Buying "designer" clothes	Finding out the hard way that you no longer have a "designer" body
Getting a toy boy/girl	Everyone will think you're their mum or dad
Finding out what the latest music is	Finding out that you can't stand it

One of the other reasons that "getting down" with the kids is not a good idea is because older people and younger people interpret things differently and you will only end up more confused than you usually are.

If a teenager wakes up wondering where they are, it's because they had a good night out and got so drunk they can't remember a thing about it. If you wake up wondering where you are, it's because your memory's not what it used to be and you can't remember anything even when you're stone-cold sober.

If a young person says something is "bad" then it probably means it's good. If you say something is "bad" then it is probably something you don't approve of because you're old.

If a teenager's phone hasn't rung all day, they assume that either it's out of order or none of their friends are talking to them. If your phone hasn't rung all day, you will assume it's either your lucky day or your hearing's going.

If an area is described by an estate agent as "vibrant" this will seem tremendously exciting and alluring to a young person. To you, it is estate agent speak for: "Here be monsters".

When a new TV comedy programme is described as "cutting edge", "controversial" or "irreverent" a young person will reach immediately for the "on" switch. You, on the other hand, will reach for your quill pen to fire off an outraged missive to the Head of Light Entertainment.

How To Turn Idling Into A Hobby

We wrinklies love to while away our leisure time and, indeed, our life's savings on hobbies. Often we will take advantage of the increasing leisure time available to us to take a sudden and intense interest in activities such as gardening, golf, photography, ballroom dancing, needlework or making sketches of naked people (ideally with the naked people's prior consent).

Alternatively we may take up a particularly challenging hobby such as learning Mandarin Chinese, rock climbing, white-water rafting or amateur brain surgery.

There is, however, another hobby that we can take up, which involves no financial outlay, minimal physical or mental exertion and doesn't even require a bus ticket to the local further education college to enrol on a course.

And the name of this hobby is, of course, "idling".

Lazing around. Wasting time. Generally getting up to not very much at all. Idling is surely the perfect hobby.

Also, when you think about it, idling is the hobby we have been gearing up to pursue our whole lives.

Remember all those days spent in your youth – whether at school or sitting bored at work – gazing out of the window? You weren't wasting your time, after all. You were in training for the hobby you intended to take up in later life.

Idling is also clearly the hobby that millions would like to pursue. Just look at them all round you every day, wandering about aimlessly with vacant expressions on their faces. Idling could be seen as some sort of preparatory study or cogitation over a highly complex mental problem. At any moment you might leap from your idling into a period of intense outward activity. However, observers might have a long wait for this.

Some people are lucky. They manage to pursue a career in idling by getting paid employment either working for the civil service or answering the phone help line at a major utilities provider or acting as president of Jim Davidson's fan club.

The rest of us have to enjoy idling on an amateur basis. But now we are in our wrinklyhood, we can devote ourselves more fully to this activity.

When friends ask us if we have any hobbies, we can proudly tell them, "Oh yes. I have a hobby. It's called 'idling'. I spend as much time as possible doing it."

We can then proudly show them what we have produced while pursuing our hobby of idling – nothing whatsoever!

Some may not be terribly impressed by this. They will argue that idling is not really a hobby and will attempt to define it instead as inertia, lethargy or complete indolence.

For such doubters it may be best to avoid using the term "idling" and describe your hobby as "meditation", "rumination" or "internal yoga".

If, however, you do choose to describe your idling as such, be careful that no-one catches you snoring and dribbling from the side of your mouth during a period of particularly intense "meditation".

How To Terrify Those Around You As You Exercise

The sight of wrinklies indulging in hard exercise can greatly upset young people at the gym, in the park or in their own homes if you live in the house opposite.

But just what do these young people find so upsetting? And, more importantly, are there any ways we can upset them even more?

Wrinklies in sportswear
Who could possibly object to seeing an ageing person in Lycra? Skin-tight Lycra is a very useful fabric for wrinklies. Particularly if their actual skin is no longer skin tight. Lycra can help a wrinkly hold everything more or less back in the places it occupied 30 or 40 years earlier.

Young people will also be disturbed by the sight of wrinklies in revealing sportswear such as swimming trunks, particularly if this is all they are wearing while going round the supermarket.

Overexertion
If a young person sees a wrinkly overexert themselves to even the slightest extent, they will immediately begin worrying that the wrinkly is about to drop dead in front of them.

Young people worry about this for many reasons: they fear having to answer awkward questions from the emergency services; they fear having to ask the wrinkly if they are all right (young people hate having to speak to anyone they don't know and will avoid this at all costs); and worst of all, they fear they might be required to perform mouth-to-mouth resuscitation on the wrinkly.

Flying off the end of the running machine
Other gym users worry when they see a wrinkly approaching
a running machine. They think he/she will set the machine at
a speed that even Usain Bolt would find difficult and will then
try to leap onto it like John Wayne jumping astride a wild
stallion in mid-gallop in an old cowboy film.

Rather than beginning to canter along the treadmill like a
gazelle speeding across the grasslands of Africa, the wrinkly
will stand for a split second looking unsure as to
his or her fate before being dispatched to the end of the
running machine belt at over 70mph and launched like a bolt
from a crossbow into the brick wall immediately behind.

Suffering a hernia
One definition of a wrinkly is a collection of lumps sticking
out at odd angles to one another. Nevertheless, the sight
of anything bulging from a wrinkly's sportswear is likely
to horrify onlookers and cause a mass exodus from the
gymnasium. Well, as they say, you can like it or lump it.

You will successfully reverse the process of ageing
Of course! This is the real reason young people don't like to
see us wrinklies exercising. They fear we may at any moment
find the long-sought key to reversing the ageing process.

We will then start to look younger and younger and
healthier and more muscular. And, of course, once we
wrinklies learn that little trick, the younger generation know
they will be finished!

The Disgraceful Wrinkly's Daily Workout

Midnight – 7.00am: Perform series of short brisk jogs or power walks between bedroom and toilet

7.00 – 7.30am: Perform series of sit-ups

7.31am: Finally manage to sit up successfully. Now you just need to get out of bed

7.31 – 8.00am: Period of intense effort – trying to squeeze yourself into clothes you grew out of in your twenties

8.00am – 9.00am: Weight lifting – carrying last night's pile of empty cans and bottles out to the recycling bin

9.00am: Carefully balanced, high-protein, vitamin-enriched breakfast – or, at least, something sufficient to give you the energy to get to the local greasy spoon for a slap-up full English

10.00am: Series of deep breathing exercises (while sucking on a series of lit cigarettes)

10.30am: More weight-lifting carrying home the daily newspaper, filled as it is with unnecessary extra sections and advertisements

11.00am: Deep intense meditation (after reading a few articles in the newspaper)

11.05am: Following deep intense meditation, compose a strongly worded letter to the *Daily Mail* readers' page on the subject of layabouts or corrupt politicians

12.00am – 2.00pm: Light lunch followed by a few slightly heavier ones to fill you up

2.00pm – 4.30pm: Period of intellectual study and appreciation of objets d'art – depending on exactly which quiz and antiques shows are on telly during the afternoon

7.00pm – 8.00pm: Power walking (from pub to pub)

8.00pm – 10.30pm: Swimming – or, failing that, drinking like a fish

10.30pm – 11.00pm: Boxing – or, at least, repeatedly getting slapped by young people at the bar to whom you have made inappropriate advances

11.00pm – 12.00pm: Excursion to the countryside – after a friend talks you into attending an illegal rave

12.00pm – 3.00am: Intense aerobic exercise – while bouncing around in a field

3.00am – 3.05am: Push ups – trying to pick yourself off the ground after collapsing incapably

3.05am – 3.15am: Brisk jog – running away from police raid

3.15am – 4.00am: Vocal exercises – loud singing on way home

4.00am – 7.00am: Deep satisfying period of restful sleep – or period of unconsciousness lying face down in your front garden

The Luge As A Means To Get Down The High Street

Extreme sports also have a practical application for wrinklies. It's very busy on the roads these days, so why not consider adapting dangerous sports as a means to get to the shops?

In winter sports, competitors in the luge travel at speeds approaching 90mph. That's significantly faster than most mobility scooters currently available.

You could luge down to Tesco's and be back with a pint of milk before the kettle's boiled!

Additionally, luge competitors travel at extraordinary speeds while lying flat on their back. They look as though they just accidentally slipped over and went whizzing around the circuit entirely against their will and better judgement.

Again this aspect of the luge will surely appeal to any wrinkly. During a walk down the high street, we feel constantly in danger of tripping on those paving stones that the council never get round to fixing. Or we may be pushed over at any moment by the masses of young people advancing towards us like a merciless army marching towards Starbucks or the mobile phone shop.

So if you're going to end up flat on your back anyway, why not embrace the fact?

Borrow a young relative's skateboard or balance yourself on a couple of roller skates, lie back and shoot down to the shopping precinct passing between the legs of other pedestrians and beneath passing vehicles.

You can tell your wrinkly partner, "I'm just popping to the luge!"

The Wrinkly's Introduction
To Bungee Jumping

• Your bungee cord should be slightly shorter than the drop you are about to jump over. Not the other way round. The importance of checking on this point will gradually become clear.

• The end of your bungee cord should be shorter than the drop you are about to jump over by at least your own height measured from head to toe.

• The end of your bungee cord should be firmly secured before (not after) you jump. Do not leave a Post-It note asking someone to tie the end of the cord to something some time after you have commenced your descent towards the ground (preferably before you reach the ground).

• Tie your bungee cord to a point at the upper level from which you are jumping. Do not tie it to something at ground level below you as though you require the elastic to pull you towards the earth at a speed slightly faster than gravity can manage alone.

• If you have a prosthetic leg, attach your bungee cord to your other leg. Unless that is also prosthetic.

• If you use a wheelchair, do not tie the bungee cord to your wheelchair. In fact, to be honest, bungee jumping may not really be for you.

• Fix your glasses, false teeth, wig etc firmly in place before jumping. Alternatively, have someone standing by below ready to collect up the shower of your detachable elements in a bucket.

Chapter 4:
Where, When and How To
Be A Disgraceful Wrinkly

Disgraceful wrinklies should be constantly on the lookout
for places and opportunities for appalling behaviour.

It's all very well saying to people that you are growing
old disgracefully but, as we all know, it is more effective to
show than to tell.

People need to see you growing old disgracefully. And
these people need to be suitably appalled as a result.

They need to see you going out to collect your pension
dressed in an outrageously inappropriate outfit; they need to
hear the thrash metal music blasting from your car radio as
you screech to a halt outside the day care centre; they need to
hear you singing rude words at the church Christmas carol
concert; and they need to be at the table in the pub next to the
one you are drinking yourself under.

Many opportunities for disgraceful behaviour can be
found in the course of your every day wrinkly life.

Why not behave shockingly at the shops, deplorably at the
doctor's, dishonourably at the discount store, offensively at
the off-licence, breathtakingly at the bingo hall, horribly at
the health centre and woefully at the well woman clinic?

Right! That's the rest of your day's appointments sorted
out for you! And at the end of all that, you could always end up
by being politically incorrect at the police station and maybe
monstrous at the magistrate's court the following morning.

Just remember, growing old disgracefully is best practised
with as much of an audience as possible. Naturally the more
disgraceful your behaviour, the larger the audience you will
attract – as many well-known celebrities will surely attest.

Luckily there are many establishments and venues that seem to have been specially created to encourage disgraceful behaviour. These include pubs, bars, clubs, discos and dance halls.

Alternatively, for those on a budget, there's always the local park or slap bang in the middle of the roundabout at the end of the high street.

You could, of course, try growing old disgracefully in the confines of your own home but this will probably prove an error. Very few will be aware of your efforts and your house will end up in a right old mess as a result of your disgraceful activities.

Eventually social services will notice that you have allowed your house to descend into a disgraceful condition and you will be removed from your own home and charged with allowing yourself to live in conditions unfit for human habitation.

And that's before we get on to the case the RSPCA will bring against you for the conditions in which you've been keeping your pet cat.

No, such solitary disgracefulness will surely not prove ideal. The joy of growing old disgracefully is to enjoy yourself to the full and to get up the noses of younger people in the process.

The order of preference for these two options is left to your own discretion.

At The Supermarket

Supermarkets and wrinklies do not, frankly, mix. Especially these new-fangled supermarkets with talking tills, ciggies hidden from sight and all the rest. To be a disgraceful wrinkly, you need to buck the system.

Unexpected item in bagging area
Yes, it's you! You've just parked your backside for two minutes while you get your breath back after lugging basketfulls of Werther's Originals up to the till, and Little Miss Robotic Bossyboots is barking out orders at you. Well, tough.

Change machines
You tip out six month's supply of loose change down the chute and out comes a ticket "allowing" you to spend it at the counter. However, it's taken a couple of quid in charges. Next time, just feed your loose change into the payment slot of the self-service till when buying groceries and save money. Try it with a real cashier, however, and you'll get the evil eye.

Hidden cigarettes
In their wisdom, supermarkets have decided that if you can't see something you won't want to buy it. Even if you've never smoked before in your life, you will feel instantly compelled to take up the habit just to stymie Big Brother and his dictatorial ways.

"Five items or fewer" express lanes
They don't specify what items though, do they? How about a 48-can pack of lager, some unidentifiable vegetable without a barcode, a Christmas tree, a bottle of Scotch that needs the plastic tag removing, and 200 loyalty vouchers? That'll keep 'em busy.

In The Queue At The Post Office

As with supermarkets, you really feel you must put a fly in the ointment, don't you? They have all these petty rules and myriad forms and interminable queues, so when you get the chance you feel that you must fight back. For wrinklies, England and St George!

Queues
A post office without a queue is like a camel without a hump, a teenager without the hump, or Bruce Forsyth without a catchphrase – unthinkable! Take a leaf out of the German tourist book and lay down your metaphorical beach towel while you go and do something more interesting for half an hour. A pretend parcel will do. If it's ticking, you will come back to find no queue at all.

Moaning pensioners
Even though you might be on the downhill section of the roller coaster of life, it doesn't mean that you will enjoy hearing other wrinklies moaning about their lot, so you have to outdo them. Whatever has happened to them has happened to you, but ten times worse. Onedownsmanship, in a word. It might even clear the queue.

Silly rules
After waiting half an hour in the queue and finding the cost of posting the birthday present to Auntie Gladys in Australia will be almost half a week's pension, you then have to complete a customs declaration. Unless the counter clerk is watching very carefully, you can amuse yourself by filling it in with complete gobbledegook. Who reads this stuff anyway?

In The Car

The car offers ideal opportunities for the wrinkly growing old disgracefully. Just the make of car can tell people much about you. Try going for anything that others will consider too fast, too sporty or too noisy for a gentleman or lady in their wrinkly years.

You can also define your disgracefulness by the size or age of your vehicle. Any extreme will do as long as it is an extreme.

So, for example, a very large 4x4 will look quite disgraceful if there is a little tiny grey wrinkly head attempting to peer over the dashboard.

Similarly a very small car packed full of a very large, overweight wrinkly will also appear quite disgraceful if not potentially unroadworthy as a result of the excess load.

A sleek sexy brand new car will be regarded as disgraceful if driven by someone who is no longer quite so sleek, sexy or brand new as they used to be.

However, it is also possible to look outrageous by persisting in driving an ancient banger that looks even older than you do and which produces even worse emissions.

Other means to drive in a disgraceful manner include frequent use of the car horn (preferably one that plays a jaunty little tune); saucy messages stuck in the back window (such as "honk if you're feeling wrinkly"); and any amount of "pimping up" (such as large rubber eye lashes on your headlamps or, for the wrinkly driver, a car-sized pair of spectacles).

On Long Train Journeys

Buying a ticket
Trying to buy a train ticket is a very complex business these days. So make sure you go through every possible option with the ticket clerk in such excruciating detail, they get so fed up and decide to buy the ticket for you.

Claiming your seat
There are two options for claiming as much space around oneself free of other passengers as possible. The first is to spread out all your newspapers, books, sandwiches, legs and other travel paraphernalia, thereby requiring other passengers to ask your permission before they can take the seat next to you. The other is to leave the space next to you completely free but then keep waving wildly to those looking for a seat in an apparent enthusiastic attempt to get them to sit down next to you.

Starting up a good old-fashioned sing song
This is a particularly fun thing to do if you are on a very long journey without any stops and find yourself in a compartment with just one other passenger (who really doesn't want to join in your sing song).

Mooning out of the window
Baring one's buttocks out of a train window as you pass a level crossing where a mass of drivers are waiting is, of course, going to get you into a lot of trouble. So why not see if you can talk that other lone passenger in the compartment to do it instead?

At The Beach

To be frank, the only thing a wrinkly needs to do at the beach to be disgraceful is take his or her clothes off. Not all of them of course, though on some beaches that might be de rigueur.

No, the sight of a wrinkly in his or her bathing costume will be enough to have everyone else running for the hills, or at least the sand dunes, in fright and horror.

If said wrinkly is not only wearing a skimpy bathing costume but is also engaged in some other activity that shows off the wrinkly flesh, such as Taekwondo or helping to form a wrinkly human pyramid or windsurfing, then all the better. Or worse, depending on whether you're doing, or watching.

Let's be honest, wrinklies and beaches don't really mix, do they?

If you were inventing beaches, and thought it would be a jolly good idea to have people wearing very little, engaging in sporty activities, rubbing oil into their skin and showing off their fabulously toned bodies, you wouldn't then think, "Hang on, there's something missing in this equation: saggy bottoms, shrivelled skin, and grey body hair", would you?

If you did, your concept would be doomed from the start. Imagine going onto *Dragons' Den* with that one.

"OK," would say some scary person in a suit. "So, you've got a sort of outdoor health club and people scampering around in the sunshine wearing not much and you want to allow wrinklies in? I'm out."

At The Cinema

Let's face it, the cinema is not a place for wrinklies. These young people come swaggering in with their supersize cartons of popcorn and gallons of cola in cups the size of coal scuttles, then sit and chomp and slurp their way through a film that is too long, has far too much swearing, sex and violence and a soundtrack whose volume turns your vital organs to jelly.

Here are a few suggestions as to what would improve the "cinema experience" for the average wrinkly:

No one under 25 should be allowed in. Ideally, no one under 55, but that might be impracticable.

Refreshments should be Paynes Poppets and Kia-Ora. Any refreshment that needs to be held with both hands is frankly preposterous.

The volume of the film should not be set at a level that could drown out a jumbo jet. Some of us wrinklies may be a little hard of hearing, but we're not that deaf!

Bring back smoking. Remember when cinema seats had ashtrays attached to them? At least if everyone is smoking fags they won't be chomping their way through half a ton of smelly popcorn throughout the film.

Shorter films. Needing a toilet break in the middle of a film is bad enough, but needing two is just plain ridiculous!

Less sex and violence. There's enough of that at home, thank you very much!

In The Pub

If you can't behave disgracefully in a pub, where can you? The pub is a place where the wrinkly should be able to let his or her hair down. And if you don't have any hair left to let down, you can let your friends down by enjoying yourself just a bit too much.

Once upon a time, the older person in the pub would be sitting in a corner playing cribbage or dominoes with a few other old fogies and nursing their pint of stout or gin and 'it'.

Today, the wrinkly has so many other ways to while away an evening at the local.

Karaoke, for example. Damn clever those Japanese. Back in the old days, you used to have a few drinks and then sing on the way home. Now you can sing while you're drinking. On stage. With a microphone. How good is that?

Also, by the time you've finished singing, the pub will have emptied and you will have a choice of seats in which to sit and recover.

And televised sport. At one time, men would prop up the bar and moan about how badly their football team was doing, but now you can do the moaning actually while the match is being played and drown your sorrows at the same time.

In the old days, women were barely tolerated in pubs, but now some of the places are like permanent hen nights.

Wrinkly men: be afraid, be very afraid.

At The Doctor's

When you find yourself at the doctor's with a waiting room full of people, why not:

• Describe your ailments very loudly in very great detail to the receptionist or anyone who will listen (possibly using photographic illustrations). Well, everyone else at the doctor's always seems to do this.

• When you are given your prescription, ask if you can have the recipe so you can try making the pills yourself from ingredients you have at home.

• Cough, sneeze and splutter consistently until you manage to clear the waiting room.

• In conversation with other patients refer to the waiting room as "Death Row" and your doctor as "The Grim Reaper".

• Tell each of your fellow patients how terrible they look and insist they better go in to see the doctor before you "while there's still time".

• Get undressed ready for examination before entering the doctor's room.

• Tell unsuspecting patients that the number displayed next to each of the doctor's rooms refers to the mark they got out of 100 in their final medical exams.

• Carry a copy of a large encyclopaedia of medical conditions in to the doctor's room with you, throw it down on the table and tell him that you have got the lot.

With People Who Come To The Door

The main daily exercise that we wrinklies get is jumping up and down to go and answer the front door to unwanted callers. Here are a few suggestions of things to say that might shut up some of the more persistent of these nuisances:

With religious maniacs:
"How nice of you to call. Please come in and let me tell you all about my lifestyle and beliefs."

With people selling household cleaning products door to door:
"My, my! A packet of dusters for only £15. How do you ever make a profit?"

With delivery men asking if they can leave a parcel with you for next door:
"No. The neighbours told me if they weren't in, you should just smash one of their living room windows and throw the parcel in through there."

With people delivering charity collection bags:
"Just hold it open while I empty the bin into it. I didn't think you usually came to collect the rubbish until Friday."

With people wanting to sell you home improvements:
"I'd quite like some sort of booby trap installed whenever anyone rings this damn doorbell."

With any hopeful looking person holding a clipboard:
"Here's a pen. Now just write the words 'Bugger off!' next to all the questions on your list."

At Family Weddings and/or Funerals

What you should do	What a disgraceful wrinkly might do
Wear smart clothing	Wear a silly grin as you over-imbibe the free booze
Make pleasant conversation with people you haven't seen in years	Make sworn enemies of people you've known for years
Congratulate the hosts on how well it's gone	Castigate the hosts for how much money they've wasted
Be on your best behaviour all day	Be on your back all day after all that free booze
Try to mingle with people you've never met before	Try to mangle people you never want to see again
Thank the vicar for a lovely service	Forget the vicar is there when complaining loudly about how long and boring the service was
Try hard to remember everyone's names	Try hard to remember your own name when completely sozzled
Remember this day is very important to someone else	Remember this is the day your favourite TV programme is on and tell everyone you're missing it
Try not to outstay your welcome	At 4am still be regaling everyone with your jokes about Englishmen, Irishmen and Scotsmen

At A Meeting Of The Parish Council

Declarations from the local parish council that suggest that at least one of its members is a disgraceful wrinkly:

• Wrinkly drivers have right of way in the village on all highways, roads, walkways and in the queue at the Post Office.

• Wrinkly drivers are permitted to park their cars anywhere in the village, including in spaces already occupied by other vehicles.

• The council hereby extends local licensing hours; instead of being allowed to serve alcohol each evening until 23.00 hours, local pubs will instead be permitted to serve alcohol until 2300AD.

• The revised opening hours do not apply to those under the age of 40, who are henceforth deemed as minors and banned from consuming alcohol by order of the council (as they are unable to hold their drink and become far too rowdy after a couple of bottles of alcopop).

• The council intends to re-introduce stocks on the village green as a means of punishment for local miscreants and ne'er-do-wells. As the village green was tarmacked over in 1957, the stocks will be positioned outside the local mini-mart (thereby providing ready access to rotten fruit and veg).

• If any wrinkly manages to throw any rotten fruit and veg at a person sitting in the stocks so it bounces off their head through the automatic doors of the mini-mart and back into the fruit and veg display within, the said wrinkly will be entitled to a full refund on their purchase.

On A Tour Of The Local Museum

A museum should be a place where you quietly and respectfully view the ancient artefacts and marvel at their antiquity, rarity and general wonderfulness.

However, seeing as you may be one of the oldest things in the place, you should be able to behave just as you damn well please.

Here are some of the things you could say as a disgraceful wrinkly:

"Call that old? I was in the prime of life when that vase/doll/ whatever was still a twinkle in someone's eye."

"I've got children older than some of the so-called antiquities in this place."

"Don't 'shush' me, young man/lady."

"What kind of museum is this if it doesn't have a tea room or a gift shop?"

"I don't have to sign a visitor's book every time I go to a public lavatory, so why should I have to sign one here?"

"Call the police – see if I care."

"They say it's impossible to sleep standing up, but I managed it here."

"If I'd have wanted to wander around looking at piles of old rubbish, I could have gone to the Tate Modern for nothing."

Chapter 5:
How To Be An Ageing
Rock 'n' Roller

Ageing rock 'n' roller? Is there any other sort?

Once upon a time, rock 'n' roll was the preserve of young men and women who wanted to rebel against adult society. And guess what, rock 'n' roll is still the preserve of that same bunch of men and women, but they just aren't young any more.

Even a relative youngster such as Bono from U2 is ten years older than both the Jedward twins combined. Mick and Keef from the Rolling Stones are each ten years older than any three members of One Direction combined!

So, in other words, you've got plenty of role models!

If there's one section of society that's always behaved disgracefully, it's the average rock 'n' roller. It's virtually written into the contract.

When rock 'n' rollers book into hotels, they don't go for the upper floors because of the view, they book them because the TV will make a much more satisfying crash when it hits the ground below.

Rock 'n' rollers are also more likely than most to perish in hotel fires – simply because they have emptied all the fire extinguishers while having 3.00am water fights or trashing their rooms. Val Doonican, they ain't.

Whether any of the above antics will be any fun while staying in a Cotswolds Travelodge is open to question, though.

Also, you have to bear in mind that rich rock 'n' rollers can afford to pay for the mess to be cleared up afterwards.

You may therefore have to set your sights a little lower. Perhaps you could just throw the TV remote out of the window?

And rather than filling the hotel bathroom cabinet with illegal drugs, you could fill it with chilblain cream, denture cleaning tablets and all the other multifarious concoctions that a trip away necessitates taking with you.

Then there is the small matter of learning to play an instrument. While it's easy to forget that certain tabloid-fodder wrinkly rockers ever actually made any music, it is, of course, the original reason that they were ever allowed to become a disgrace to society.

In fact, you don't really have to learn to play anything. Even if you don't get as far as the O2, just wandering around with a guitar slung round your neck will give you carte blanche to make an exhibition of yourself.

He hasn't shaved? Oh well, he's a rock musician. She's wearing green nail varnish at her age? Well, she is in a band...

You can get away with almost anything.

Just don't let anyone hear you play any music. When was the last time you heard a decent tune from any of these superannuated superstars? Exactly.

"Here's a song from our new album" is enough to clear any arena.

As Elvis once said, "I don't know anything about music. In my line you don't have to."

A Day In The Life Of The
Wrinkly Rock 'n' Roller On Tour

• Wrinkly rock 'n' roller wakes up surrounded by groupies after a night-long orgy of drugs and hot sex.

• Groupies inform wrinkly that he nodded off before the orgy began and so missed all the good bits; not only that, his snoring was slightly off-putting for the other orgy attendees.

• Wrinkly rock 'n' roller starts to feel bored; decides to throw television out of hotel window.

• He realizes television is slightly heavier than thought and calls down to room service to ask for someone to come up and help him throw the TV out of window.

• Wrinkly rock 'n' roller realizes *Antiques Roadshow* is on; attempt to throw TV out of window is temporarily abandoned.

• Wrinkly rock 'n' roller climbs astride and revs up his Harley-Davidson mobility scooter before setting off for tonight's gig; he gets two yards, realizes the scooter is still plugged into the charger; he unplugs it and sets off again.

• He arrives at massive stadium ready for tonight's show.

• He is informed that he has come to the wrong place and that he is playing in the function suite of the Royal British Legion club next door.

• Wrinkly rock 'n' roller arrives at gig; plugs in his guitar to his Marshall stack and turns volume up to 11; can't hear a thing; realizes he has left his hearing aid back at the hotel.

The Wrinkly Rock 'n' Roller's Tour Dates

These days, there's no money in the business of selling records. This is because young people don't have record players, they don't have money and they don't have any taste in music, either.

People now get all their music downloaded from the internet, although some genius (probably a wrinkly) has worked out another way exists in which people can download music – through the air during a live performance.

So what are the likely venues to be played by a wrinkly rock 'n' roll act today as they hit the road on tour with the avowed intention to have "No Sleep Til Hammersmith!" (as a result of their recurrent bladder problem)?

Glastonbury Festival
Reading Festival
Little Thatch Walton-on-the-Naze Flower Festival
T in the Park Festival
Tea in the local park
Isle of Wight Festival
Mr and Mrs Hedges' B & B, Isle of Wight
Woodstock Festival (New York State)
Woodstock Antiques Festival (Oxfordshire)
Radio 1's Big Weekend
Saga Radio's Moderately Sized Weekend
Monsters of Ear Splittingly Loud Monstrously Noisy Really Very Loud Indeed Rock Festival (acoustic stage)

And basically any other festival where the organizers have installed a Stannah stair-lift to help the acts get up onto the main stage.

The Wrinklies' Guide To Achieving The Effects of Illegal Drugs By Entirely Legal Means

Cannabis

Cannabis is said to provide its users with a relaxed half-awake state and has a strong funny smell. Wrinklies clearly don't need illegal drugs to achieve this sort of thing. An episode of *Midsomer Murders* will provide the relaxed half-awake state and the funny smell comes as standard in many wrinkly homes.

Heroin

If you become addicted to heroin, you will end up looking pale, feeling terrible and having no money whatsoever. Again this is quite similar to the state in which many wrinklies normally exist. This particularly applies to those trying to survive on a state pension. Heroin is also said to give you a warm feeling like being wrapped in cotton wool. So clearly the wrinklies' legal equivalent to heroin is a nice snug foot warmer or one of those blankets with armholes.

Speed

A brand new extra fast mobility scooter is probably your best bet for this one. If you can't afford that, just put your old one on the top of a steep slope with the brake off.

Cocaine

An expensive white powder, which you snort and which gets your heart racing and makes you worked up and excitable. For similar effects, why not try a pinch of snuff while scanning the readers' letters page in the *Daily Mail*?

Smoke And Be Damned –
How To Foil The Health Fascists

If you don't smoke, then maybe it's not a good idea to take it up just to be bolshie, though the temptation is always there in these politically correct times. And far be it from us to try to promote smoking – that may well be a hanging offence these days. But if you do smoke and have no intention of giving up, then you might as well enjoy it instead of pursuing it as a guilty pleasure on a par with fox-hunting or listening to Buck's Fizz records.

Test the law
Presumably, if you never exhale, then you're not polluting the air in any given building. Similarly, if you smoke outside but keep one lungful of smoke to exhale when back inside the building, can that be constituted as "smoking in the building"?

Electronic cigarettes
These sound about as much fun as electronic chocolates. Avoid.

Start a smoking club
The sheer joy of throwing out non-smokers would be a huge pleasure in itself.

The Euthanasia argument
Why is it that you can go to a Swiss clinic to bump yourself off quickly, but if you want to do it the slow, fun way with booze and fags no one will let you?

The Pot argument
Why is it that smoking dope is almost legal, while smoking fags is almost illegal?

Inventive Ways Of Having
Yet Another Drink

Just because you're retired, people think you're sitting round
all day knocking back the cooking sherry at any excuse. And
if you're not retired they suspect that the first thing you do
when you get home after a hard day is to crack open the
Tom Cruise. Well, "people" may be right.

Now you don't want to get a reputation as an inveterate
boozer, do you? The red nose can be put down to a genetic
skin condition, the wobbly gait to old age, the slurring
of words to dodgy dentures and the permanent state of
confusion to, well, being a wrinkly.

So, any excuse for a guilt-free tipple should be welcome.

The sherry trifle
What could be more homely and traditional? Well, one with
an entire litre bottle of sherry in it – but who would know?

Wine gums
Of course wine gums don't contain wine, but they do if you
marinade them overnight. Pinot noir for the blackcurrant ones,
rose for the strawberry ones, chardonnay for the lemon ones…

Communion
Yes, the vicar may start to get a bit suspicious when you've
been up seventeen times and are bumping into pews on the
way back to your seat, but despite being bang out of order
you will also feel strangely virtuous.

A few more assorted excuses for sneaking in that extra tipple:

• Look at your watch and declare that it is opening time (well, whatever time it is, it will be opening time somewhere around the world).

• Look at your watch again and declare that there is just time for one more quick one before closing time (it will be just coming up to closing time somewhere else around the world, so again this method could help keep you drinking constantly for the rest of eternity.)

• Claim that you are on a personal mission to single-handedly clear the national debt by means of alcohol duty contributions.

• Tell people you are drinking to forget but there still seem to be one or two things left that you are able to remember.

• Claim that you are helping to save a friend from alcoholism by drinking their share of the world's booze for them... before they are born.

• Say that you are just having one for the road – so far, you have had a drink for all the roads up to and including the A432 to Chipping Sodbury.

• Say that you have to drink a toast to Bernard Higgins because it's his birthday today. (OK, you don't know who Bernard Higgins is, but once again, somewhere around the world there will be someone called Bernard Higgins and it will be his birthday today.)

Doing Wrinkly Things In A Rock 'n' Roll Way

At a certain point in your life, you will find yourself doing all those things that you laughed at your parents for doing. Wearing sensible shoes, visiting National Trust homes and looking forward to "nice cups of tea" and sit-downs. But it doesn't have to be that way. With a little tweak here and there, you can still find new twists on those time-honoured wrinkly pursuits.

Normal wrinkly pursuit	Rock 'n' Roll version
Buying pot plants	Growing "pot" plants
Painting the living room	Painting the town red
Having an afternoon nap	Having an afternoon nip
Curling up on the sofa with a good book	Curling up on the sofa with a complete stranger
Getting out to a stately home	Getting your home into a state
A cream tea at three in the afternoon	A party at three in the morning
Wearing leather elbow patches	Wearing leather biker boots
Proudly baking rock cakes	Loudly making rock music
Caught kipping on the beach	Caught skinny-dipping on the beach
Liking rambles	Biking scrambles
Putting your feet up	Having a rave-up
Easy listening bringing on nostalgia	Easy listening bringing on neuralgia

Items Demanded By Wrinkly Rock 'n' Rollers On Tour In Their Contracts

• Champagne, port, burgundy, claret, sherry – and any other flavours of wine gums that you can find available;

• Twenty crates of vodka, fifteen magnums of champagne and twenty crates of rum. But if that's not possible a large pack of tea bags, milk, sugar, kettle – oh and a tin of cocoa as well, please, for after the show;

• Plentiful supply of glass tumblers plus full container of Steradent tablets;

• The services of a masseur, physician, chiropractor, chiropodist and fully qualified hip replacement surgeon (in case of fall occurring during show);

• An abundance of hard drugs, including opiates, stimulants, hallucinogenics and nasal decongestant spray (a doctor's prescription for all these will be presented on the night);

• Plentiful supply of warmed massage oil and/or Vicks Vapour Rub and/or Tiger Balm;

• Full buffet of organic fruits, vegetables, nuts, pulses and syrup sponge pudding with custard for afters;

• A hot tub – but if that's not possible a plug-in foot warmer;

• A bowl full of all the brown M&Ms that Van Halen's riders have been asking to have removed from their bowls of M&Ms over the years – waste not, want not!

The History Of Wrinkly Rock 'n' Roll

It is a well-known fact that the great rock 'n' rollers are now all extremely wrinkly. Many of these great rock 'n' rollers of the past are, however, still rocking 'n' rolling today (albeit slightly more slowly than they used to and with some creaking and cracking now thrown in for good measure).

There is, of course, a very good reason why the great rock 'n' rollers of the past have to carry on rocking 'n' rolling even at their greatly advanced ages. And this is because there are no great rock 'n' rollers of the present!

Let's face it, a latter-day teenage heartthrob like Justin Bieber is no Jerry Lee Lewis. Justin Bieber might be slightly more in the right age range for one of Jerry Lee Lewis's wives, but let's not go into that.

Instead the great old rock 'n' rollers of yesteryear have to keep going simply in order to show the youngsters how it should be done. Would this state of affairs be tolerated in any other profession?

Are there any other jobs where the complete incompetence and inability of the younger generation to take up the mantle forces 70-, 80- and even 90-year-olds to carry on working till they drop?

Would people be happy to see 80-year-old coal miners forced down the mine and made to keep working into their dotage just because the youngsters aren't up to the job? And yet analysis shows that rock 'n' roll, rather than being the preserve of the young, has always been geared towards the wrinkly generation.

Rock 'n' roll is, after all, noisy enough to be heard by slightly deaf wrinklies and repetitive enough to appeal to wrinklies with extremely poor memories.
But what of the early pioneers of rock 'n' roll? Could they also have been pursuing the wrinkly audience?

Bill Haley was no spring chicken even in the 50s and one of his hits, "Shake Rattle and Roll" was clearly dedicated to wrinklies everywhere (particularly those who had been prescribed large numbers of pills by their doctors).

Although he died young, Buddy Holly clearly attempted to appeal to the wrinkly audience by his constant wearing of thick-framed glasses.

Fats Domino evidently named himself after a weight disorder familiar to many wrinklies and a popular wrinkly leisure activity. This was considered such a good idea that Chubby Checker decided to do exactly the same thing.

Chuck Berry is still rocking today (at the time of writing) although he now needs some assistance being held up while he performs the duck walk and may eventually need to invest in some form of duck-themed mobility scooter or a Stannah duck lift.

And even Elvis himself was initially known as Elvis the Pelvis in clear reference to hip operations so beloved of wrinklies, while his habit of shaking his hips was, contrary to popular belief, surely an attempt to avoid the onset of varicose veins.

Tonight We're Gonna Party Like It's 1959!

Yes, by all means get down and roll back the years to the days when you had to roll back the carpets to party, but why not form a band and lay down some music for your generation? Here, to get you started, are some names you could use:

Gran Funk Railroad
Geriatric and the Pacemakers
Oldie and the Gingerbreads
The Hip Replacements
The Grandmothers of Invention
Wrinkly Floyd
The Methuse La's
The Specs Pistols
Creaking Clearwater Revival
The Old Spice Girls
Old-Codger-Goo-Goo
OAPsis
Paul McCartney and Bingo Wings

Or if you fancy going solo:
Granny Lennox
Wiggy Pop
Grey Charles
Rickety Astley
Bandy Newman
OAPete Townshend
Wrinkly Hazelwood
Grum P. Diddy Fogey Carmichael
Seniley Minogue
Ill. I. Am

And a few of the songs you could do:
"Ovaltine-age Kicks"
"Going Down the Dustpipe (and slippers)"
"Money's Too Tight in My Pension"
"Wake Me Up Before You're Gaga"
"I Want Your Specs"
"Aged and Confused"
"Creak Out!"
"Grey Balls Of Fire"
"Senile Friends"
"Stairlift To Heaven"
"The Gin Crowd"
"Walking Frame In Memphis"

And even some classic albums:
Sergeant Pepper's Cronies' Darts Club Band
Dicky Fingers
Bus Station To Bus Station
Songs For Whingeing Lovers
Travelodge California
A Night At The Soap Opera
Ex Lax On Main Street
Kind of Blurred
What's Going On? I'm Confused
Ever a Dull Moment
Goodbye Yellow Thick Hair
Wish I Could Hear

Rock 'n' Roll Role Models

If you want lessons on how to be a disgraceful wrinkly, look no further than the gossip columns when they include superannuated superstars. Have they no shame?

At a certain age, the drugs a wrinkly might be taking could include Sanatogen and sleeping pills. Not crack cocaine and speedballs.

Remember when people used to look at the disgraceful antics of long-haired pop groups and put it down to the follies of youth?

Well, that argument started to leap out of the window like an LSD-crazed rock star when those young, long-haired yobbos were no longer young and in many cases no longer had any hair, let alone the long variety.

Without naming names, you will have read about wrinkly rockers who now have girlfriends younger than their own daughters.

For a male wrinkly to achieve this himself, he will first need to accumulate a fortune in excess of, ooh, give or take a few quid, maybe £20,000,000.

For a female wrinkly to grab a toy boy, she will need not only the £20,000,000 fortune but also another few million to spend on regular facelifts, tummy tucks, boob jobs, wigs, posh frocks and all the rest.

Harsh, but true. For some reason, ageing male rockers can get away with a face looking like a relief map of the moon with a jet-black wig stuck on top of it. If they've got the ackers, they get the crackers.

Wrinkly women, unfortunately, not only have to have a million dollars, they have to look like a million dollars, too

– and that doesn't mean green and wrinkled. If you aren't rolling in it, though, you may be able to tell your friends you now have a toy boy or toy girl at home – without letting on it's your grandchildren's Ken or Barbie, which they left behind on their last visit.

And then there are the other antics wrinkly rebels get up to:

Punching photographers
Being harassed by the paparazzi 24/7 must get quite irritating, so you can see why some stars lash out. This might not be quite so easily excused, though, when it's the official photographer at your granddaughter's wedding.

Getting thrown out of nightclubs
Simply being a wrinkly (without the mitigating factor of piles of dosh) will be quite sufficient to get you chucked out of any self-respecting nightclub.

Dangerous stunts
Whether it's Sir Dickie Branson in hot-air balloon hell, or some dopy rockstar crashing his private plane, there are a variety of ways people old enough to know better can make fools of themselves. Attempting wheelies on your mobility scooter should do the trick.

Rehab
Being seen going in and out of clinics may well be part of your weekly routine now anyway. Don't let on it's for your dodgy knees, just say it's a twelve-step drink and drug programme.

Inappropriate Times And Places To Play Loud Rock Music

The wrinkly rock 'n' roller loves playing the classic tunes of his or her youth at full volume. These days, it's usually the only way a wrinkly can manage to hear them properly. Nevertheless there are times when it will be considered extremely rude or unhelpful to get out the wrinkly ghetto blaster. Which, of course, a disgraceful old wrinkly rock 'n' roller will consider absolutely ideal.

So just what are the worst (or best) times to put on your old Who, Led Zeppelin, Deep Purple and Black Sabbath LPs or just Cliff Richard's Greatest Hits and crank the volume up to 11?

With your wrinkly partner:
While they are trying to tell you something really important.

While they are on the phone.

While they are attempting to comfort a quietly spoken friend or relation who is in a state of evident distress.

While they are squatting on a cushion in the next room trying to have a session with their relaxation and meditation group.

While they are suffering with a really bad hangover.

While they are sitting in the same room attempting to listen to their own old (but much quieter) acoustic LPs.

With your children:
Whenever they have popped round to try to talk you into giving them a bit of money.

With your neighbours:
Just when they've managed to get their children off to sleep.

Just as they're getting off to sleep themselves prior to an early start for work the following morning.

At the moment you hear the theme music from their favourite TV show starting up through the wall.

While they are attempting to perform some activity involving serious mental effort, such as filling in their tax return, revising for an exam or trying to work out how to assemble a flat-pack wardrobe.

A couple of moments after they finally get their dog to stop barking.

While they are having a tense argument.

While they are showing round some people who are (or, perhaps more accurately, were until recently) interested in buying their house.

Generally bad moments to turn up the music:
At funerals – particularly those of close family members or at which you are presiding in some official capacity.

In hospital – particularly while a surgeon is performing a tricky operation on you or a loved one and, as a result, is having difficulty being heard when requesting items of surgical equipment.

During marriage guidance counselling sessions.

When being presented to the Queen.

Chapter 6:
The Oldest Swingers In Town – The Pursuit Of Wrinkly Romance and Hanky Panky

The pursuit of love in later life is often considered disgraceful by others. This is, of course, an extremely unfair and uncharitable response. The older generation are as entitled as anyone to love, affection and emotional and physical fulfilment. And that applies even to those of us who are particularly ugly.

On the other hand, if you stumble across a pair of wrinkly old octogenarians attempting to get a bit of physical fulfilment from one another, you might be shocked and startled. But there again it would be your own fault for wandering into their bedroom unannounced.

People scorn us wrinklies for wanting to find love. They seem to believe that we should have grown out of that sort of thing years ago and content ourselves instead with more appropriate hobbies and pursuits.

It is a mystery why anyone expects wrinklies to behave like this but not any other age group. No-one ever suggests that sex-crazed 20-year-olds should try to alleviate their urges by taking up gardening, needlework and lawn bowls.

There are many reasons why a wrinkly might feel the need to go out and seek love. A wrinkly may, for example, have suffered the loss of a partner or realized a deep-seated need for emotional attachment.

Or perhaps the wrinkly concerned has just had one or two drinks too many and suddenly fancied his/her chances with the barmaid or barman.

And now there are plenty of ways in which it is possible to meet new people with less risk of embarrassment, rejection or threat of arrest by the police than was the case in the past.

Online dating is one of the most popular means by which people find love today. Many internet sites exist offering this service. They're a bit like eBay, but rather than offering for sale bits of old rubbish that no-one wants any more, they list *people* who nobody wants instead.

Speed dating is another modern means of seeking a companion. This involves having a series of very brief chats with a series of potential partners seated at a series of small tables. It's like a dating version of musical chairs.

Some wrinklies may find the "speed" element of the proceedings to be a challenge and will spend the greater part of their "speed dates" heaving themselves up and plonking themselves down in a series of chairs.

Nevertheless, speed dating is ideal for wrinklies in other ways. These days a five-minute conversation with a stranger will tell a wrinkly everything he or she could ever possibly want or need to know about them.

So today all of us wrinklies should be able to find love and companionship and there needn't be any disgracefulness involved.

Although for those who do want some disgracefulness involved, alternative services do exist and these are also relatively easy to find on the internet (or so we are told).

Chat-Up Lines For Wrinklies

"So tell me, gorgeous – do I come here often?"

"When I saw you, my heart missed a beat. Mind you, that happens quite a lot if I don't take my pills."

"When I look at you, the places where I used to have hairs on the back of my neck stand on end."

"Hey, baby, is it hot in here or is it just you? Or is it just you having a hot flush?"

"You look so sweet, you give me toothache.... Or at least you would if I had any of my own teeth left."

"We were made for each other. Well, we were made in the same century as each other."

"It would be wonderful if we could walk along holding hands together. For a start, we'd need one less walking stick each."

"Come on, baby, let me take you up to the stars on my stair-lift to heaven."

"So which is it going to be, darling? Your care home or mine?"

"Let me shout sweet nothings quite loudly, slowly and clearly into your ear trumpet."

"I can't quite reach to nibble your ear, but if I pass you my dentures will you do it for yourself?"

Classified Ads For Wrinklies

So just what do all those abbreviations that people use in classified singles ads really mean? And do they mean anything different when a wrinkly uses them?

Abbreviation	Normal meaning	Meaning for wrinklies
BB	Body builder	Bent and broken
BBW	Big beautiful woman	Badly behaved wrinkly
DF	Drug-free	A dribbling fossil
FWB	Friend with benefits	Fantastically weather-beaten
GF	Girlfriend	Greatly feeble
GSOH	Good sense of humour	Good sense of hearing
HWP	Height weight proportional	Has wrinkles perpetually
IPT	Is partial to	Inanimate prehistoric type
LDR	Long-distance relationship	Listed decaying relic
LTR	Long-term relationship	Long in tooth and rickety
MBL	Married but looking	Methuselah but longer-lived
NM	Not married	Not modern
NSA	No strings attached	Neglected, senile and ancient
OHAC	Own house and car	Old, haggard and creaky
TV	Transvestite	Toothless veteran
VGL	Very good-looking	Very geriatric lover
WE	Well endowed	Wrinkly everywhere
WLTM	Would like to meet	Wrinkly lady terribly moth-eaten

Excuses Used By Those Seeking
A New Partner In Their Wrinklyhood

Two can live as cheaply as one
A wrinkly will often attempt to woo another wrinkly with
this economic based argument. The theory is that two people
will be able to live more economically together as a couple
than they could separately.

How romantic! It's the 'two for the price of one' approach
to love. It's the argument that says, 'We may not find each
other particularly attractive but think of the money we'll save!'

And of course this may be absolutely true. If nothing else,
you can save on heating bills by huddling together during the
winter. This does mean, however, that if you and your new
partner fall out, you may be replaced by a convector heater or
a foot warmer. Financial savings can also be made on other
household purchases including food. On the other hand you
could always just get yourself a pet dog. A canine companion
will also finish off your leftovers for you, it will keep you
much warmer than a bony old wrinkly and it won't argue
with you about what to watch on TV.

Social security advantages
It is true that some pension benefits exist for married rather
than co-habiting couples. Nevertheless it's probably best
to avoid anyone who announces on a first date or during a
marriage proposal that the main reason they're interested
in a relationship is the social security benefits.

Unless they just need help filling in the forms.

We can look after each other in our old age
Don't fall for anyone giving you this excuse either. This declaration of romantic intent is most likely to be made by those who have just discovered that they are completely incapable of looking after themselves and require 24 hour care (despite having absolutely nothing wrong with them).

This may have happened as a result of the recent loss of a partner or perhaps a sharp increase in fees at a local domestic cleaning service. 'We can look after each other in our old age' may actually translate as 'You can look after me starting with immediate effect.' It may not be so much a romantic overture but an offer for you to work as an unpaid care assistant into your dotage.

Think of the tax benefits if we get married
There may be tax advantages in being married but that still doesn't make it a particularly romantic reason to propose!

'I didn't fall in love with you when I looked into your eyes nor after our first date nor after we had spent some time together but then when I sat down to fill in my tax return form I definitely began to feel some stirrings.'

Companionship
This is quite a good reason for seeking a partner at any age although you should beware of anyone who makes this offer because everyone else they have ever known during the course of their life is no longer prepared to speak to them any more.

Places To Meet Footloose Fogies

If you are looking for love, you don't want to go to the sort of place where young people think you're only there to complain about the noise. Insults such as "coffin-dodger" or "dirty old man" are not going to put you in the required frame of mind for wrinkly romance. Therefore you need to go to the right places.

Clubs
Nightclubs, by definition, are way past your bedtime anyway, so find clubs where people have similar interests – e.g. moaning about young people, watching TV programmes about antiques and wondering what the world is coming to.

Garden centres
Once upon a time a garden centre was where you bought plants. How dull. Today the garden centre will have a nice café, possibly licensed, where you can hang around like some horticulture-hungry lounge lizard or femme fatale and sweep members of the opposite sex off their poor tired old feet. Ding dong!

Bus stops
Driving around in your sensible saloon may be more convenient and possibly give off a marginally exotic whiff of wrinkly independence, but who on earth are you going to meet?

The bus stop, however, is a veritable speed-dater's dream. You have 101 cast-iron excuses to talk to other people. The flippin' weather, the flippin' buses, the other flippin' passengers, flippin' kids… If you can't chat to someone at a bus stop, you're a doomed cause.

The post office

In the days when you could still collect your pension from a post office, there was no better place to meet the wrinkly of your dreams.

Of course, those government busybodies and killjoys soon put a stop to that. However, seeing as you will probably spend a good 25 minutes waiting to obtain a humble stamp, that will give you ample time to do your "social networking".

Walking the dog

You don't have a dog? Well, get one. Can't afford it? Then start a dog-walking service and get paid for it. As you will have observed, it's only wrinklies who ever walk dogs.

Young people are far too busy/lazy/cool to hike the hound. You will find that as your dog and somebody else's dog engage in mutual sniffing of the physical variety, the owners will be metaphorically sniffing around each other with romance in mind. Woof woof!

Your own front room

How so? The passing parade of possible partners is surely at a minimum in your own humble home is it not?

Well, at the moment, yes, but set yourself up as a therapist or a life coach or something that doesn't need any of those pesky qualifications and you will have a steady stream of wrinkly lovelies swanning in and out of your boudoir, er consulting room, before you can say, 'But I'm innocent, your honour!'

Dream Dates For Romantic Wrinklies

When you're younger you have certain expectations and requirements for the perfect date, but when you reach your vintage years things change, as we can see from the table below:

Younger person's dream date	Wrinkly's dream date
Women want a tall, dark handsome man	Wrinkly women want a man who still has his own teeth
Men want a pretty young woman with a nice figure	Wrinkly men still want a pretty young woman with a nice figure, but will settle for anyone who will have them
Someone who can make them laugh	Someone who can make them laugh, but for the right reasons, not simply by undressing with the light on
Someone who's a good listener	Someone who can still hear
Someone who dresses well and keeps up with fashion	Someone whose clothes are largely post-war
Someone who looks after their body	Someone who doesn't look after the body of every young person who happens by
Someone who shares their interests	Someone who doesn't only want to share the interest on their savings
Someone who shares their taste in music	Someone who shares their interest in "turning that bloody racket down"
Someone with sparkling conversation	Someone who is still awake at the end of the evening

And it's not just who you meet, it's where you meet them which can make or break the perfect date.

Again, the requirements of wrinklies differ slightly from those of younger people.

Younger person's dream date location	Wrinkly's dream date location
A smart restaurant where you can push the boat out	A cheap restaurant where it's a set price with no hidden extras
A trendy nightclub with pulsing music	A pub with a "pipe down!" policy
A concert starring some cutting-edge new band	A concert featuring some band you thought had all died in the 1960s
A day having fun at the dry ski slopes	A day having fun by doing nothing at all
A day at a theme park	A day at a theme pub
A weekend in a boutique hotel on the coast	A weekend in a B&B on the cheap
Driving off and having no idea where you are going	Driving off and having no idea where you are going (but not for the same reason)
Cooking a candlelit dinner at home	Microwaving a TV dinner and watching *Downton Abbey*
A last-minute impromptu weekend in Paris	A last-minute impromptu cinema trip when you find it's half-price
A trip in a hot-air balloon	A trip on a bus just for the hell of it using your free pass

What Not To Wear On A Date

What we wrinklies need is a bit of fashion advice. We don't want to be going out as mutton dressed as lamb or even horse dressed as beef.

In other words, we can't really be tarted up like young flibbertigibbets, because frankly, our gibbets are rather a long way past the flibberti-ing stage.

If we go out on a date, it must be done with decorum, taste and dignity.

What we need is a sort of older version of Gok Wan. A venerable sage of fashion – a sort of Gok Wan Kenobi if you will.

While we're waiting for that, here are a few dos and don'ts:

• Do dress to impress. Don't undress, because that won't impress.

• Ladies, don't wear miniskirts. The term "mini" means they probably won't do them in your size anyway.

• Men, your role model may once have been Marlon Brando in *The Wild One*, but if you wear that peaked cap now women will think you're an off-duty milkman.

• Don't try wearing those low-slung trousers because your actual bottom may now be too far down for them to decently reach.

• Don't try to dress younger than you are. Oh, go on, then, but not younger than 50.

• Don't wear tight clothes. At your age your circulation needs all the freedom it can get.

• If you think something looks "cool", definitely don't wear it.

And in case you're still confused, here are a few more important things you should avoid wearing when you go out on a date again:

• The same lucky outfit you wore last time you were dating in 1978 and which has been sitting at the back of the wardrobe ever since (waiting to be washed and/or to come back into fashion).

• The same underwear you've had on for a few days (particularly if you're wearing them over your outer clothes).

• Anything that hides your face such as a hoodie, a full face mask or a balaclava (stop worrying what you look like – you can't look that scary... or can you!?)

• A tee-shirt printed with an insulting or over-saucy slogan (e.g. do not turn up on your date's doorstep in a tee-shirt with "I'm with stupid", "Come and get it, ladies!" or "Hello, boys!" printed on the front in large letters).

• The same outfit you wore on your wedding day (your date may take this as being ever so slightly presumptuous).

• Whatever you normally wear in the evenings (don't go out on a date dressed in your saggy elastic sweatpants or pyjamas).

• A tee-shirt you had specially printed with a large colour portrait of a much loved but sadly recently departed former partner.

• Any outfit made entirely from skin-tight rubber.

Mood Music For Courting Wrinklies

When a wrinkly couple are lowering the lights, slipping into something more slinky and preparing for an evening of romance, they do not want their ears assaulted by "music" from some so-called "rap artist" (was there ever a better example of an oxymoron?).

Nor do they want the dulcet strains of Lemmy from Motörhead bellowing out from their Wharfdales. They don't want Acid Jazz, Trip-hop, Death Metal or any such other awful racket shaking the chandeliers and curdling the Harvey's Bristol Cream.

Choosing the right music is an integral part of the wrinkly seduction technique.

If music be the food of love, let's not end up with indigestion.

Also, certain sorts of music which may be all right for youngsters to canoodle to are perhaps a bit too racy for wrinkly sensibilities.

To be honest, even that Jane Birkin record was a bit spicy. "Je T'Aime Moi Non Plus"? Well, some of us certainly were non-plussed. If we want to hear heavy breathing, we can just try running up the stairs, thank you very much.

And as for Barry ("Walrus of lurve") White, well…!

No, wrinkly wromance wrequires (*Oh, stop it! Ed.*) something a bit more subtle.

And here are a few suggestions:

Acid indigestion jazz:
The aural equivalent of a couple of Alka Seltzers. Gentle, soothing, and almost noiseless.

Crock 'n' roll:
A bit like rock 'n' roll but… well, in fact, nothing like rock 'n' roll at all. Because although that was all very well when you were seventeen, your "wopbopaloobop" simply refuses to "lopbamboom" anymore.

Light industrial noise:
Some rather strange Germans invented a style of music called "industrial noise" which mimicked machines. Well, for the wrinkly the gentle sound of a boiling kettle or the ping of the microwave is far more welcome.

Psychedelia Smith:
What wrinkly wouldn't feel a surge of passion at the sound of Dame Delia reciting recipes to a backwash of ambient music?

Old Romantic:
Well, New Romantic is out for obvious reasons and this will be just perfect!

Slipped disco:
Key words here are "energetic" and "not". You get the picture.

Old Age music:
Like New Age, only even quieter.

Chapter 7:
The Art Of Offending
Everyone You Meet

To be a truly disgraceful wrinkly, you have to know how to offend people. To some, this comes naturally; for others, a little guidance is needed.

Now we're not saying you should go around offending everyone just for the sake of it – that job description is more suited to an E number-chomping adolescent. We all have our places in society.

No, this is more a case of payback. Payback for all the little indignities and insults you have to suffer day to day at the hands of rude youngsters, officious public servants, doctors' receptionists, your wrinkly other halves et al. (Ooh, isn't that an annoying, pretentious phrase? We thought we'd just pop "et al" in to show how easy it is to annoy people without really trying). So here goes:

Doctor's receptionists
See how we put that apostrophe in the wrong place just to annoy you? Anyway, you know how sometimes when you go to the desk and the receptionist studiously ignores you as you cough discreetly and shuffle your feet? Well, there's one surefire way to get their attention. Simply say, 'I think I'm going to be sick!' If you can actually be sick, then all the better.

Young people
Surly, sweary, scruffy... you may think some young people hold all the trump cards in the gentle art of offence, but no, you have the ultimate ace up the sleeve, which they simply cannot match.

Just being old is really enough to offend any youngster. If, however, you can raise the stakes by removing your false teeth, showing them wrinkles that are normally kept from sight, etc, then game to you.

Officious public servants

Your car is parked with its wheels slightly on the pavement, your privet hedge has outgrown the boundaries of your "dwelling" ("house" in plain English) and is 10mm over the "public footpath" (pavement), your alcohol intake is over the recommended number of units (tots). When they ask for your name just say, "Bugger off" and when they get shirty explain that you have Russian ancestors and it's actually spelt "Buggerov".

Your wrinkly other half

Do you really need any advice on how to offend your wrinkly other half? You are no doubt a past master or mistress at it and should probably be giving everyone else advice.

The rest of the known universe

If, as Professor Stephen Hawking suggests, we should soon be colonizing other planets, you need to hone your offending skills for all eventualities.

Offensive language – The words "Little", "green" and "men" are sizist, racist and sexist. All boxes ticked!

Who knows, the inhabitants of other planets might live to be 5000 years old. This means that the boot will be on the other foot and you can make rude remarks about their age – what a welcome change!

If all else fails, on this planet, or any other, just be yourself. That should be enough to offend everybody!

Offensive Things A Wrinkly Can Do Without Having To Say Anything

The truly disgraceful wrinkly has to be ultra-versatile, ever vigilant. Any old fool can speak his or her mind – which is usually enough to upset anyone of a sensitive nature. But the inventive disgraceful wrinkly will have a whole armoury of other apple-cart upsetting wiles up their cardie sleeve.

For example: Wrinkly women can sit with their legs firmly apart à la Les Dawson in public places and cause even the most fearless of hoodies to avert their eyes.

Wrinkly men simply have to forget to tend to their personal grooming for several days. The resultant unruly tufts of ear, nose, and Heaven-knows-where-else hair will cause everyone, including even battle-hardened wrinkly women, to drop their jaws in horror.

Every wrinkly, whether male or female, can perfect the art of dropping off to sleep anytime, anywhere. The sight of their lolling, and possibly dribbling, mouth hanging open like a puckered Venus flytrap will be guaranteed to offend almost everyone. This is especially effective in smart restaurants.

It's a well-known fact that at a certain age, wrinklies don't give a Jonathan Ross what people think of them. This is particularly true of the clothes they wear. If cold, they will wear dreadful combinations of hats and earmuffs, caps with flaps, goggles – like a cross between John McCririck and Sherpa Tenzing. Especially not a good look if you're a woman.

If it's hot, wrinklies will be tempted to display more than is decent of their wrinkly flesh – and let's face it, any amount of wrinkly flesh is far from decent. Either that or they will be putting hankies on their heads, fitting those attachable sunglasses things on their normal glasses, rolling up their trousers or finding another 101 ways of offending anyone with even a passing acquaintance with dress sense or personal dignity.

Even without the excuse of extreme weather, the wrinkly will find a way of dressing in such a way as to make even the merely middle-aged avert their eyes. Grim shades of grey or beige, muddy hues of depressing brown, light-swallowing bottle greens and even the dog swaddled in faded tartan – it's enough to offend anyone.

At times, even the forthright wrinkly will realize that there are certain things which simply cannot be uttered in these enlightened times. It is at this point that the often underrated curled lip will come into play. Whether it's the thump, thump, thump of teenage music or the extremes of fashion favoured by the young, or perhaps someone extolling the virtues of mass immigration, the curled lip will speak a thousand wrinkly words.

When all else fails, the wordless utterances of the wrinkly digestive system will offend most within earshot. The silence-shattering tummy rumble, the involuntary belch (or worse) should suffice in maximum offence for minimal effort.

Excuses That Can Be Used For Giving Offence In Old Age

"I'm sorry you were upset by what I called you. I didn't realize the term 'ugly great moose-faced twerp' was no longer socially acceptable."

"I'm sorry. You misunderstood me. I didn't mean to be rude to you. It's just that you reminded me of a great hairy baboon I knew in my youth."

"I'm sorry I shocked you by telling you that you were ugly. I presumed you'd know already."

"I'm sorry I upset you with my language, but words have changed their meaning over the years. When I was young the phrase 'pathetic useless completely incompetent dollop of inanity' was often used as a term of endearment."

"I'm sorry I upset you when I called you a 'blundering malodorous dunderheaded buffoon'. I didn't realize you'd be intelligent enough to understand."

"I'm sorry. It was completely wrong of me to call you an ugly, bald, greasy ignoramus'. My eyesight is rather poor and I can now see you do still have a little bit of hair."

"I'm sorry. It was insensitive of me to call you 'a fat, ugly, great red-faced gorilla'. I can see now it's a genetic problem inherited from your mother."

The Wrinkly's Guide To Which Topics Are Most Likely To Raise The Hackles Of Which People

Type of person	Suitably offensive topics of conversation
Wrinkly partner (female)	Their weight; their appearance; their dress sense; the weight, appearance and dress sense of someone who looks similar to them but who is slightly younger
Wrinkly partner (male)	Their weight; their appearance; the strange odour they leave behind them when they pass through a room; their ineffectiveness at DIY; their lack of a sense of humour; their lack of hair
Your children	Detailed inventory of how much you've had to spend on them over the years; how much you're going to cost them in your old age
20-year-old	Their sex life; your sex life; the early onset of wrinkles; the early onset of baldness; the early onset of weight gain; the early onset of no sex life
30-year-old	The official definition of when middle age begins
40-year-old	A detailed account of the physical and mental decline that they will experience over the next few years
Next-door neighbour (on left)	The way they park their car; the noise their children make; the noise they make while shouting at their children; the fact that none of their children resemble their father
Next-door neighbour (on right)	The way they park their car; the noise their children make; the noise they make while shouting at their children; the fact that their children resemble your other neighbour

Ways In Which To Claim Offence

Apart from giving offence, wrinklies are also very good at taking it. But that's what life's all about, isn't it – a little give and take?

Like Martini, offence can be taken any time any place anywhere. Put a wrinkly on a desert island, completely alone and he or she will find something to take offence at: 'Only the Bible and the complete works of Shakespeare? How dare they!' Even a racy plotline in *The Archers* is enough to raise the wrinkly hackles. Umbrage at Ambridge is fast becoming a wrinkly blood sport.

It goes without saying, of course, that wrinklies will constantly be offended by their wrinkly other halves and other family members. That, surely, is part of the job description. But when they are not around, the sensitive wrinkly will find slights and offence aplenty in the most unlikely of places:

"How can that newsreader read a royal story wearing a green tie? Disgraceful!"

"Wallace and Gromit on postage stamps? Whatever next!"

'Yes, they've put the pension up, but only by 40p! It's not even much in old money!'

"Flipping raining again! It was never like this before we joined the Common Market."

"Cheeky young blighter – offered me his seat on the bus. What does he think I am – decrepit?"

Opinions That You Really Shouldn't Hold

The world isn't what it once was, and even if it were, you would not be a wrinkly and would not therefore be reading this book. You'd be young, opened-minded and tolerant.

However, by the time you reach wrinklyhood, you will find that your views have changed somewhat.

You no longer think, "live and let live". You think, "Why is everyone else having all the fun and how can I put a stop to it?"

We all read of those once anti-establishment types who are now "Sir" this or "Dame" that and the extreme left-wing political firebrands who are now donning the ermine in the House of Lords.

And so it is with the wrinkly. We can't be anti-establishment forever; it's far too exhausting. But as our views become increasingly out of synch with the rest of society, we have to keep them to ourselves – or slightly adapt them.

Instead of complaining about immigrants, complain instead about parakeets. "Flippin' green so and so's – why don't they go back to their own countries?"

Instead of complaining about women bishops complain instead about male bishops wearing frocks. "I'm not going to be preached at by anyone in a dress."

By using these sorts of diversionary tactics, you will find that you can still offend people but stay on the right side of the law. Just about.

Taking Legal Action
Against Everyone You Meet

Thank goodness for legal aid! Once upon a time, you had to be loaded to be able to sue someone, but now you can do it on a pension. And what with small claims courts, and ambulance-chasing lawyers egging you on to sue everyone in sight, it really can put the spring back into the step of even the most wronged-against wrinkly.

Restaurants
The chances of finding glass in your goulash, fingernails in your fish fingers or mouse-droppings in your moussaka are probably quite slim, so always remember to take your own and put your acting skills to the test as you work up into a frothing lather of self-righteous indignation and suddenly "find" them in your food.

Shops
Half of what you buy these days falls apart in five minutes anyway, but you also need to be inventive in finding something to complain about when things are working perfectly well. Such as, "This 'magic eye' book you sold me does not work by magic!"

Hotels
The hotel is, of course, a complainant's paradise. Uncomfy beds, rooms too cold, too hot, too stuffy, too draughty…
　　If you can't find something to get a reduction on your bill, you should be ashamed of yourself.

Everyone else
As a wrinkly, you are officially a "minority". You have rights. Assert them.

Tradesmen

Show us a plumber, painter, builder who has ever done a job perfectly and we'll show you an unobservant wrinkly who doesn't deserve their day in court.

Bus companies

Fortunately for the wrinkly, the bus is a veritable death trap. With careful planning, he or she can get off the bus just as the doors are shutting and catch their cardie sleeve in them. The looks of horror on the faces of the other passengers and the mobile phone footage caught by a wrinkly accomplice as the bus drives off will ensure that even a free bus ride can be a nice little earner. Hold tight, please!

Local councils

It's hardly necessary to make anything up for this lot, is it? With the loose and wonky paving stones looking like there may have been a minor earthquake in the vicinity recently and with faulty traffic lights, pedestrian crossings that require the speed of a Usain Bolt to beat the bleeps, and 1001 other hazards and irritants, you could book yourself a season ticket for the local magistrates' court if you fancied it.

Passers-by

In these litigious days, it should be perfectly possible to take somebody to court if they give you a "funny look".

You obviously can't rely on that, so if you see the same person more than once you should probably be able to make a case that they are stalking you. It might be stretching the local magistrates' credulity, though, if the "stalker" is 40 years younger than you and quite attractive.

How To Find The Bad In Everyone

There is a fine art to this. Whatever anyone else is doing, enjoying or wearing, you can find something wrong with it. However innocent, however charming, it takes but the blink of a gnat's eyelid for you to condemn it. Observe:

Harmless Activity	Wrinkly Interpretation
Children playing football in the street	They are deliberately trying to smash your windows and should be publicly horsewhipped
Young lovers kissing on the doorstep	They are clearly passing drugs to one another by mouth and you are even now speed-dialling the local police station
A young man is helping an old lady carry her shopping	A young thug is blatantly stealing a harmless old lady's groceries
Two policemen are patrolling the street together	The crime is obviously so bad round here they're scared to go out alone
A young mum is buying her toddler an ice-cream from a van	Typical modern parent force-feeding her child junk food. Probably hasn't given him a square meal in weeks
Man across the road is washing his car	We all know his car's bigger than anyone else's, but he has to keep on showing it off?
House next door is having groceries delivered	Too posh to shop! Who do they think they are?
Woman at door is collecting for charity	It's obviously all a front. Probably fund-raising for terrorists
Man down road is wearing new hat	Obviously found a bald spot. Must share this information!

And it's not just what they do, but what they say as well. Keep those wrinkly antennae tuned to a fault:

Innocent Remark	Wrinkly Interpretation
Lovely weather we're having!	He wants to borrow my strimmer!
And how are you today?	Someone's been blabbing about my angina/knee/whatever's giving me gyp again
How's the family?	They've all been plotting behind my back to have me put into a home!
Have you got the time, please?	They want to steal my watch. It's obvious – they're wearing hoods
Can you sign for this parcel for next door?	I get it! When the police/Inland Revenue/Customs and Excise investigate, it'll be my name on the form!
Happy birthday	Rubbing it in about my age again
You're looking well	They make it sound like the exception to the rule. That's nice.
You must come round for dinner	Obviously got a new kitchen to brag about
Pleased to meet you	How much do they want to borrow?
Unexpected item in bagging area	They're accusing me of shoplifting! Flipping cheek!

What Your Personal Habits Say About You

Our wrinkly other halves are constantly irritated and maddened almost to the point of committing wrinklycide by our little habits, but where's the challenge in that? Any wrinkly worth his or her Epsom salts will be able to tell the world something about themselves (and irritate the hell out of it) by simply displaying those little habits that just come naturally.

Wrinkly Habit	Meaning
Scratching head	This is a Freudian way of saying to the world: I may be old, but I've still got some hair left. Look, here it is!
Working the jaw in a chewing-like motion when not actually eating	I may not be capable of doing much exercise these days, but at least I can keep my mouth in working order
Whistling tunelessly	Being tone-deaf has not stopped half the pop stars on this planet performing, so I'll be damned if it's going to stop me
Biting fingernails	Not only do I have hair, I have teeth too!
Saying "aaaaah" every time you sit down	You are, of course, not truly speaking at all, but the sheer effort of sitting down actually winds you
Constantly jiggling foot up and down	Everyone's got to have a hobby!
Constantly checking and rechecking you've turned lights off	You have OCD (Over Charging Dread)

How To Earn A WASBO (That's A Wrinkly ASBO To You) Without Really Trying

OK, at the moment, the WASBO is only a figment of our fevered imaginations, but surely it's only a matter of time.

The average wrinkly is just as capable of getting on the wrong side of the law as some young hoodie – and you can't plead that it was a youthful indiscretion.

Inadvertent shoplifting
Shopping these days is such a kerfuffle, what with loyalty cards, automatic tills, cashbacks, remembering to bring bags, school vouchers, money-off vouchers and all the rest, it's so easy, after faffing around with all that, to forget to pay. Well, it is, isn't it, your honour?

Traffic violations
Your eyesight's not what it was, neither is your hearing, so it's very easy to misinterpret a "no priority lane" as an advert for the Red Arrows or the terrified scream of a pedestrian as a shop alarm, so really, you can't be held accountable. Can you?

Being a Peeping Tom (or Thomasina)
Those binoculars are, of course, merely part of your personal "neighbourhood watch" kit. The fact that you are using them 24/7 and exclusively spying on your own neighbours is neither here nor there. At least, that's your defence and you're sticking to it.

Kerb crawling
It's very difficult to do anything else on a mobility scooter. Isn't it, your honour?

Chapter 8:
Turning To Crime
In Later Life

It's never too late to turn over a new leaf. Just because you've been obeying the law all your life doesn't meant to say you have to carry on doing so.

Where has it got you, quite frankly? You've been toeing the line, doffing your cap, playing by the rules all these years and you're harder up than ever. And we need criminals. If we didn't have them, what would all those scriptwriters and novelists write about?

And who will suspect you? When was the last time you saw a wanted poster with a mugshot of a little old lady with white hair? Or a gent with a flat cap and Boots off-the-peg specs?

Plus you have your unblemished record of 60+ years which the court will take into account if you are actually nicked.

"Your honour, my client has been a fine, upstanding member of the community for the best part of seven decades, is vice-president of the bowls club, works every other Wednesday afternoon in the charity shop and is a founding member of the local Neighbourhood Watch scheme – this, surely, was a moment of madness." What jury could possibly send you down?

You will also be able to blame your failing eyesight, dodgy hearing and less than reliable memory as mitigating factors.

"I picked up the Securicor case thinking it was my handbag. I realized my error only when I noticed the security guard was still chained to it.'

"Yes, I did drive off in this gentleman's Bugatti Veyron, but it was parked right next to my Reliant Robin – who hasn't made a similar mistake?"

Also, after a lifetime of being ripped off by banks, utility companies, dodgy builders and pension providers, you may not even look on what you're doing as crime.

It is surely just a redistribution of wealth. You are a wrinkly Robin Hood, taking from the rich and giving to the poor – which just happens to be you.

You may decide to set up as a team. You and your wrinkly other half becoming a sort of superannuated Bonnie and Clyde cruising around the country armed to the teeth with walking sticks and handbags and striking fear into the hearts of every bank that had the temerity to give you half a percent interest on your hard-earned savings while paying themselves multi-million pound bonuses.

Of course, you may not wish to go to such extremes.

You may go in for something gentler such as feeding parking meters with tap washers, or bigamy.

And if you do end up in jail, think of the money you'll save on heating. And food. And TV, and everything else. It's a wonder there aren't more wrinkly recidivists inside.

Go on, it'd be a crime not to.

The Advantages Of Being
An Elderly Criminal

• People don't tend to notice us wrinklies. This means you
can go round committing crimes left, right and centre as
though you were the invisible wrinkly!

• If people do notice us wrinklies, they often think we all
look the same and have difficulty telling us apart. If you turn
to crime, this may result in the police issuing an arrest warrant
either for the actor Richard Wilson or for the late Dame
Thora Hird.

• The identikit picture of you put together by the police may
turn out to be oddly flattering (because their identikit system
will not include in it facial elements that are anywhere near as
wrinkly as you are).

• It will be difficult for the police to trace you via any
fingerprints you leave behind at the crime scene, as these
will be covered in wrinkles.

• It will be difficult for the police to trace you by means of
any items left behind at the crime scene as we wrinklies pride
ourselves on always tidying up and never leaving any litter.

• It will be difficult for the police to trace you by means of a
pair of spectacles left at the crime scene if you remember not
to say, "I've been looking for those everywhere!" when they
present them to you.

• Forgetfulness works as an excuse for crimes such as
shoplifting – it's less effective as an excuse for crimes
such as cold-blooded murder.

• You will quickly rise to the top of any crime syndicate or gang you join because as a wrinkly you will be much better at organiszing things than any of the younger members.

• Similarly, if you have to write a ransom note or any other note demanding that a quantity of cash is handed over, this will be better spelt, punctuated and expressed than any of your younger criminal associates will be able to manage.

• Because of your age, people will never suspect you are an evil criminal (though they might begin to suspect if you are pointing a gun at them and demanding the combination number of their safe).

• You are less likely to be convicted for evading justice – in any chase situation, it probably won't take very long for the police to catch you.

• People will feel sorry for you if they think economic hardship has forced you to turn to crime in your old age (i.e. they will feel a bit less sorry for you if they discover you have become the godfather of a major drug smuggling operation using your luxury yacht).

• If you get sentenced for a really long period in prison, you probably won't get through all of it.

• You've been telling people for years that prisons are cushy joints these days – it'll be like being sentenced to a holiday camp for the rest of your life.

• Alternatively just look at prison as being like a retirement home – but one with all your fees paid for you.

Types Of Crime Unsuited To Wrinklies

Crimes under cover of night
When wrinklies turn to crime, they much prefer to do their dirty work during daylight hours.

This is because they can't see so well at night, they like to be tucked up nice and cozy at home in the evening and they are also a bit scared to go out after dark because there are far too many criminals around these days.

Ram-raiding
Ram-raiding involves a robbery on commercial premises by smashing through its front using a vehicle driven at high speed.

This method doesn't work well for wrinklies. Using a mobility scooter to try to smash through a brick wall or a plate glass window will inevitably destroy the scooter. It will also leave the wrinkly criminal lying on the pavement powerless to get away before the police turn up (because their mobility scooter has just been involved in a severe accident).

Even if a wrinkly owns a car, the process will still not work. The wrinkly car will sustain far more damage than the building it is being driven into (even if this is only a small flimsily constructed kiosk). In fact, the wrinkly car probably won't even reach the building because it will fall apart in the run-up as soon as it mounts the kerb.

The police will also be able to tell when a group of wrinklies are ram-raiding a Post Office because they will line up their cars in an orderly queue outside.

Cat burglary

Dressing head to toe in a skin-tight black outfit, scaling the side of a tall building and slipping in through a tiny gap in a high window will not suit many wrinklies.

For a start, they won't feel comfortable squeezing themselves into a skin-tight black outfit and will try clambering up the building dressed in an overcoat and scarf.

And even if the wrinkly gets part of the way up the side of the building, he or she will have to keep climbing back down again every time their hat or cap blows off.

The wrinkly will also inevitably draw attention to their intended crime if he employs someone to install a stair-lift up the outside of the building concerned.

House-breaking

This is not advised for wrinklies if the house has a burglar alarm. If the wrinkly is a bit deaf, he will not notice that he has set the burglar alarm off and that it is loudly blasting out.

The wrinkly may then emerge from the house with his bag of swag and find that all the neighbours from the other houses in the road have come out to see what is going on while several police cars and vans are in attendance and a police helicopter is hovering overhead.

The shock of this may be enough to cause the wrinkly burglar to keel over with heart failure if he or she hasn't already knocked themselves over swinging the bag of swag over their shoulder.

Ways In Which Wrinkly Criminals Can Evade Justice By Disguising Themselves

Not wearing your glasses
Wrinklies assume that no-one will recognize them if they take their glasses off. This is a misapprehension based on the fact that once wrinklies remove their glasses, they can no longer recognize themselves in the mirror (for the simple reason that they cannot see that far).

Unfortunately, just because you see a blur where your face should be does not mean that other people see the same thing. On the other hand, this method of disguise has worked for over 70 years for Superman and his bespectacled alter-ego Clark Kent.

Nevertheless, if a wrinkly attempts to commit a crime without their glasses on, they will spend their time fumbling around, knocking over and breaking any items they intended to pocket.

Stocking pulled over head
This form of disguise may again prove disastrous for wrinklies. The choice of the wrong denier rating will make it impossible for wrinklies to see out of a stocking.

The prevalence of tights these days may result in a wrinkly criminal having to work joined at the neck to an accomplice like a pair of Siamese twin criminals.

Worst of all, a stocking pulled tight over a wrinkly face may stretch all its wrinkles out, causing them to disappear and making the wrinkly look many years younger than is actually the case. Rather than disguising them, the stocking will enable police to identify the wrinkly from photos taken many years earlier.

Disney character mask

Many criminals use Disney character masks to disguise themselves in an apparent attempt to make their victims believe that they have been held up by Mickey Mouse or Donald Duck.

This ploy will not work for wrinklies, however, as they will keep revealing their identity by lifting up their masks because they need to blow their nose. Also beware that the Disney company is legendarily litigious and if you, for example, steal a million pounds while wearing a Mickey Mouse mask, they will claim the money from you because of breach of copyright.

Old man mask

Some bank robbers disguise themselves using rubber masks depicting a hideous old wrinkled face. Obviously this is a pointless means of disguise for a wrinkly. A wrinkly could put one of these old man's face masks on and look no different to the way he looks without it.

A wrinkly can instead try robbing a bank without any mask at all in the hope that everyone will presume that he is a much younger man wearing a mask. If, however, anyone mentions that the wrinkly's face is the most hideous mask he has ever seen, the wrinkly may become a bit depressed.

Full-face balaclava

The danger for any wrinkly using this method to hide their face is that the woolly balaclava may be a little too warm and cosy. This may cause the wrinkly to nod off during his bank raid and wake up in police custody.

Why Life Inside Prison Might Suit Wrinklies

Being locked in
Wrinklies like to lock the doors of their homes in the evening so they can be safe and sound. They feel the need to do this because there are so many criminals and ne'er-do-wells around these days.

In prison, someone locks your door for you and takes very great care of the key. And just to make it even safer, they lock you in from the outside so there is no danger of you going to bed having forgotten to lock your door. On the downside, you will probably find yourself locked in a small room with a load of criminals and ne'er-do-wells.

Food and drink are provided
OK, it may be a load of tasteless grey slop, but any wrinkly will be quick to point out that he has eaten much worse in his time and it certainly beats the value frozen range of foods available from the local supermarket. Besides, even grey slop tastes better when someone else has made it.

Educational opportunities
Prison offers a range of opportunities to study new subjects and acquire new skills. To a wrinkly, prison is a bit like being locked inside a college offering further education classes. Fantastic!

Opportunities to see live music
There isn't a wrinkly alive who doesn't love the music of Johnny Cash. There must surely be a range of tribute acts touring the nation's prisons performing the classic songs of the Man in Black.

You may be incarcerated for several years
This will also suit many wrinklies, as they probably did
not have much on and would have been staying in anyway.
Prison saves wrinklies having to go out in the cold and wet.
Admittedly it's probably going to be a bit parky inside a
prison cell with only bars for a window but, on the plus side,
think what you'll save on heating bills and council tax!

*They put something in your tea to sublimate certain
urges (allegedly)*
At their age, many wrinklies will have no need to have their
urges sublimated. On the other hand, if they do still have
urges they may be relieved to have them sublimated so they
can get on with concentrating on the telly or a good book.
The main thing is that the chemicals used to sublimate
these urges are being served up in great steaming mugs of
tea. Lovely!

Prison visiting hours are very restricted
What a relief! When you're at home, visitors will be people
trying to get you to switch your gas and electricity supplier
and annoying members of your wrinkly partner's family. Very
few of these will seek you out in prison.

*You'll be held somewhere out on the moors miles
from anywhere*
For many wrinklies, this will bring back happy memories
of going camping with the boy scouts or girl guides. It's just
that this time the wrinkly's fellow "scouts" and "guides"
will be huge, bald and heavily tattooed.

Excuses That Wrinklies Can Try And Get Away With When Caught Red-Handed Burgling Someone's Home

"I'm sorry, officer. I am a bit confused and I have wandered into this palatial mansion because I thought it was the two-bedroomed flat where I live."

"Thank goodness you came, officer. The people who live here kidnapped me many years ago and have been living off my pension ever since."

"Hello, officer. I live nearby, so the owners asked me to pop in and look after their cat… while they were out at the shops for ten minutes."

"I'm sorry, officer. I suddenly felt a desperate need to go to the toilet so I had no choice but to smash my way in through the upstairs bathroom window of this large and sumptuously decorated executive home."

"I'm sorry, officer. I seem to have wandered in here by mistake and I thought the only way to get out was through this small metal door in the wall that requires a combination number to open it."

"I'm sorry, officer. I think I have taken a wrong turn. I was looking for the library, but I seem to have ended up by mistake in this huge locked room full of valuable antiques."

"No, officer, I am not a burglar. I am the wrinkly ghost of a former owner of this large house."

Things That Wrinkly Criminals Should Remember When Holding Up A Bank

• When performing an armed raid on a bank, it is not necessary for you stand in the queue for half an hour waiting for your turn to go to "cashier number four, please".

• Avoid standing in the queue with your gun visible in your hand ready for the hold-up. People around you may notice and raise the alarm. You will attract even more attention if, while waiting, you stand reading the instruction manual for your firearm.

• Do not present a note demanding bank staff hand over money in the form of a letter with your name neatly printed at the bottom and your full address, including postcode, at the top.

• Do not ask the bank staff to hand over so much money that you are physically incapable of carrying it out of the bank.

• Do not hand the money back because it is too heavy to lift and ask for it to be paid into your current account instead. They may be able to trace you through your bank details and come and ask for the money back a few days later.

• Avoid holding up a bank where you have been a regular customer for several decades. This might be the one occasion where a member of staff actually recognizes you. There again, these days you'll probably get away with it.

• If you use telephone banking, attempting an armed hold-up over the phone will not be effective.

Age-Appropriate Crimes
For Wrinkly Wrong 'uns

Certain crimes are a young man's game – and it is usually men who are shinning up drainpipes, sawing the ends off shotguns and all the rest, isn't it?

And for wrinkly women, it might be quite tough to make a living out there in the red-light districts – unless the lights happen to be switched off at the time.

No, we have to face facts here; if a wrinkly wants to start flouting the law at their time of life, they have to find their own individual way of doing it. For example:

Hot-wiring mobility scooters
If they will leave them sitting tantalizingly outside day centres, what do they expect? Have you seen the price of those things? And the beauty of nicking one of these is that the owner is hardly likely to give chase, are they?

Counterfeiting bus passes
You remember when you first got your bus pass and how everyone laughed? Well, they were soon laughing on the other sides of their faces when they realized how much money you were saving. Those youngsters in their fifties would pay good money for one of these little beauties.

Become a prescription drugs dealer
Now that you are getting all your prescription drugs free, the contents of your bathroom cabinet are probably now worth more than your house. Who could blame you if your front room becomes a sort of crack den for herbal tonic addicts?

Bootlegging booze
Just when you find you've got plenty of time on your hands to indulge in a bit of imbibing, you realize that a gin and tonic in a pub will cost about half a week's pension.

If you can't knock this stuff up in your wrinkly kitchen at the dead of night and flog it to your wrinkly friends, then you're missing a trick. In the still of the night indeed.

The Gas Liberation Front
Did you know that some wrinklies spend more than half their money on keeping warm? With the aid of a hacksaw and a bit of spare pipe, you can simply reroute your gas supply so it doesn't actually register on the meter.

The only downside is that you may possibly blow up your entire street, but hey ho, desperate times need desperate measures. Good luck!

Bigamy
As if one wrinkly partner wasn't enough! But each additional one brings with them another state pension. If they're over 80, it's even more.

Of course, if the thought of a houseful of pensioners gives you the collywobbles, then you can simply forge a few pension books and tell the authorities you're running a care home and kindly administering the financial affairs of the residents for them.

You'll not only be able to bask in the warm glow of do-gooding, you'll be able to bask in the warm glow of having piles of cash!

Laws That You Break Regularly Anyway

Some wrinklies are born disgraceful, some achieve disgracefulness, and some have disgracefulness thrust upon them. You have probably been becoming more disgraceful year by year without even realizing it. Congratulations!

One day you were an upright, law-abiding subject of Her Majesty, then bit by bit you became the not-so-upright, in fact slightly stooped, shyster that breaks the law without even knowing it.

• Driving too slowly. You spent your younger years driving too fast and now you've gone to the other extreme in your cautious dotage. There must have been a point in the middle where you were actually obeying the speed limit!

• Talking on your mobile while driving. It's no excuse to say it was one of your children phoning to tell you to drive safely.

• Carrying an offensive weapon. To you it may be a walking stick, but some people would just see it as a long, thin, curly-topped baseball bat.

• Loitering. Your excuse is that you've just stopped for a moment to get your breath back. Try telling that to the young PC whose arrest levels are down a bit this week.

• Threatening to kill someone. The fact that the potential victim is an MP you have never met, the "entire bloody council" or your wrinkly other half is neither here nor there.

• Jaywalking. In the UK, we can cross the road anywhere, but if you're on holiday in Florida, you get what's coming – literally!

The God-grandfather

In the film *The Godfather*, Marlon Brando portrayed Don Vito Corleone, the patriarch of a sprawling family of criminals who are constantly fighting, getting into trouble and having to go away on holiday to Sicily.

Don Corleone could be any wrinkly with a large number of children and grandchildren. If you have a family of young miscreants and ne'er-do-wells, you may as well move into the organized crime business and try and make a few bob from the situation.

Younger members of a wrinkly's family will seem like hopeless wastrels incapable of holding down a job. In desperation a wrinkly may consider setting up a crime syndicate to provide his grandchildren with regular employment. OK, they may end up serving life sentences or worse, but on the positive side, it will stop them from turning up at the wrinkly's house every five minutes looking for a cash handout.

In event of trouble, these days they may be sent away to Ibiza or Magaluf rather than Sicily while things cool down.

Wrinklies will also identify with Marlon Brando's quietly spoken almost unintelligible delivery in the film. Presumably Marlon also had to spend his time shouting himself hoarse at other members of the family and suffered with badly fitting dentures.

Another scene from the film will surely strike a chord with many male and female wrinklies who have woken up in the morning, thought there was a horse's head in the bed next to them and then realised it was their wrinkly partner snoring away.

Chapter 9:
Disgraceful Food and Drink

Food and drink are essential to enable us to move around and remain active.

Ironically many of us fill ourselves with so much food and drink we end up incapable of movement or being active at anything.

Food and drink thus offer a range of opportunities to the wrinkly who wishes to grow old disgracefully.

You can stuff yourself with food. You can drink yourself silly. You can eat all the things you know you shouldn't and drink so much you behave outrageously.

What could be more disgraceful?

And it doesn't stop there. If you want to show people that you're growing old disgracefully, all you need to do is eat your dinner in front of them.

To be truly disgraceful, just sit there merrily stuffing yourself before their eyes making a mess without a care. You can burp, you can fart, you can smear your food all over your face, gurning cheerfully at them all the while. Of course, this may mean that they will never invite you round to their house for dinner again.

Nevertheless, all of us require food and drink to survive. Well, all of us with the exception of certain supermodels.

And yet food and drink are more than just the basic mainstays of life. They are things from which we can derive great pleasure and satisfaction. Unless, of course, we leave them out of the fridge a bit too long and they start to taste funny. Food is, for many of us, a source of intense sensual pleasure. This can derive from its taste, its appearance, its smell or just by seeing someone spill it down their suit in front of you.

But food and drink can be sensitive subjects in civilized society.

In primeval times, food was acquired by hunting and gathering. It is now acquired by going to the supermarket. This also involves hunting and gathering.

You gather your pile of money-off coupons before setting off to the supermarket, where you hunt desperately to find the specific items on the shelves from which you can get 20 pence off.

And the extraordinary range of food available at the supermarket itself provides opportunities for disgracefulness. Why not try and make other shoppers audibly gasp as you fill your trolley with clinking bottles and sweet and creamy delights?

If your till assistant feels the need to give you a few words of health advice as she checks out your shopping, then you know you really are growing old disgracefully.

There are now easy ways for you to select the most disgraceful foods available in your local supermarket. These days, many products feature a traffic light system on their packaging.

A green traffic sign means that the food is healthy and good for you. A red traffic light sign means that it is quite unhealthy and is likely to cause a traffic jam in your digestive system, if not bring your arteries to a complete standstill.

The Unhealthy Ingredients Diet

We are constantly being told by government health experts that all the things we enjoy eating and drinking are extraordinarily bad for us. Somewhat inevitably, all the things that are good for us are not so pleasant to consume. Whoever said that God doesn't have a sense of humour?

And yet we've managed to survive as long as we have, stuffing ourselves with rubbish. So we must conclude that these health experts don't know what they're talking about. Not only that, they usually look suspiciously well fed. And not on salad leaves and bean sprouts.

Nevertheless, we wrinklies will regularly be presented with long, detailed diet sheets by our grim-faced doctors. These will consist of three columns. The first will be headed "things you should eat more of". This will consist of things that we would never eat because they sound disgusting and they wouldn't fill us up properly.

Column two is headed "things that you should avoid eating" and lists all the things we live on every day.

The third column is headed "things you must avoid eating at all cost". Under this will be listed all the treats that make our lives remotely bearable.

Reading the diet sheet will be so depressing that we will spend the rest of the day trying to cheer ourselves up by stuffing ourselves with everything listed in the third column.

But just what are the unhealthiest foods for wrinklies and why exactly are they so bad for us?

Saturated fat

It's fat but saturated with even more fat. Who would have thought that would be bad for you!? Although saturated fat is very unhealthy, it tends to be hidden away in the ingredients lists printed on the bottom of food packaging in a font size too small for the wrinkly eye to read.

Manufacturers tend not to advertise the presence of saturated fat or to sell products with names such as "Saturated Fat Fingers", "Saturated Fat Escalopes" or "100% Pure Saturated Fat". You may have a problem if you are now thinking, "Why don't they do that? They all sound really yummy!"

Sugar

Sugar contains calories but no vitamins or minerals and will thus leave you feeling deflated and grumpy. And yet we wrinklies like eating as much of the stuff as possible, presumably under the misconception that vitamins and minerals are quite bad for us.

We seem to find sugar irresistible, but it does us no good whatsoever and seems completely unavoidable. It's like the culinary equivalent of TV reality shows.

There is even a TV reality show that stars someone called Lord Sugar. And guess what? He is possibly the wrinkliest, grumpiest man you ever saw.

E numbers

These are additives that are added in large quantities to food to make it more colourful, longer lasting and of interest to chemists. E numbers are clearly unhealthy for you, as they were invented by someone who was so stupid they thought "E" was a number rather than a letter.

Inside The Wrinkly's Kitchen Cupboard

The ultimate wrinkly kitchen cupboard belonged, of course, to Old Mother Hubbard. (Isn't it lucky, by the way, that her name rhymed with "cupboard" or we would never have had one of our most enduring nursery rhymes?)

But unlike Mother Hubbard, your cupboard is far from bare. If the poor dog wanted a bone, he might be out of luck, but if he wanted a year's supply of "Lucky Pup" dog food he'd be one happy bunny chaser.

Why is it that we wrinklies stock our cupboards as if Armageddon is just round the corner?

It's all very well to know that in the event of a nuclear war we would have enough food to survive for a year, but that ignores the simple fact that if there were a nuclear war we wouldn't be here to eat the food. Not to mention the fact that said food would be blasted over three different counties before you could say "four-minute warning".

Part of it is, of course, that, by necessity, we wrinklies usually have to watch the pennies. If there's a "buy one, get one free" deal going, we'll be there brandishing our loyalty cards and filling up our trolleys like mad things.

The fact that it's then going to cost us £10 to get all this extra food home in a minicab is ironic, but you never know when you might need that extra packet of cranberries do you?

No, the wrinkly kitchen cupboard is an Aladdin's cave of special offers, cans of this and that for "emergencies" and half-empty jars of stuff which it would be "criminal to throw away when half the world's starving". So, come with us as we open the wrinkly cupboard with a resounding "creeeaaakkkk".

Special offers
Oscar Wilde said he could resist anything but temptation.
You know exactly what he meant, don't you? Two jars of
caviar for the price of one? It'd be daft not to!

Emergency food
No wrinkly has ever specified what kind of emergency they're
providing for, but whatever it is it will end in the consumption
of several dozen cans of soup and baked beans. This, of
course, might result in an emergency of another sort.
Hence the accompanying emergency supply of toilet tissue.

Posh food
Some wrinklies have a slightly not-quite-thought-through
notion that the Queen might suddenly turn up unannounced
one day. It is therefore incumbent upon them to have some
"nice biscuits" stashed away for such an eventuality. When
Her Majesty fails to turn up, the wrinkly can consume the
posh biscuits in a guilt-free orgy of self-indulgence.

Lurkers
This category of food includes half-empty jars of pickles
left over from Christmas, exotic baking ingredients and
decorations for cooking projects which you never quite got
around to and various spices that "sounded nice" but remain
resolutely unopened. Naturally, half this stuff has to be taken
out regularly so you can get at something you actually need.

A Wrinkly's Guide To Warnings On Food

These days, food packaging is covered with printed information. Before eating anything, you are expected to sit reading this for half an hour to make sure the tempting treats inside the packet are not going to kill you as soon as you sink your gnashers in. The information is also always printed in tiny letters. This is because manufacturers are constantly trying to get rid of piles of terrible old food that no-one else wants by getting it eaten by wrinklies who can't see very well.

But just what do these food warnings mean?

Use by
This one seems vaguely threatening. It's as though wrinklies may receive a knock on the door in the middle of the night from officials who had been driving by in some kind of Food Detector Van. They detected a packet of French Fancies in the vicinity that remained uneaten a few hours after their "use by" date and have come to bring the wrinkly responsible to justice.

But, of course, this is a completely surreal, ridiculous and unbelievable scenario. No wrinkly would ever leave a box of cakes uneaten for more than a quarter of an hour after it arrived in their house.

All wrinklies are engaged on a never-ending mission to ensure the world's biscuits and cakes are consumed safely before their use by dates.

Best before

Packaging often informs wrinklies that their food purchases are "best before" a certain date. How do the manufacturers know this? How did they find out the precise moment at which the food would suddenly go off?

If you crept downstairs to view the item at midnight on its "best before" date, would you see it suddenly crumble before your eyes into a pile of inedible mould?

The "best before" date is also worrying to us wrinklies. If they started putting it on people as well as food, we might have to have the words "best before April 1979" inscribed somewhere about our person.

Display until

It is confusing for us wrinklies that so many food items sold today have a "display until" date rather than a "best before" or an "eat by" date.

If you spot a "display until" date on something that you have bought, does it mean that you have to place it prominently in your front window until the date shown so that people passing by can see it?

Does it mean that you have to display it on some sort of revolving plinth or will just an ordinary plate suffice?

And if some wrinkly guests pop by when you have a "display until" cake in the house, are you within your rights to bring it out, show it to the assembled multitude and tell them, "I'm sorry, but I can't allow you to eat any of this lovely cake at the moment. I'm only allowed to display it to you until the date shown."

If so, that could be quite useful!

How To Deal With Tummy Trouble

One problem with eating and drinking disgracefully is that sooner or later your tummy will start to complain about what you're doing to it.

Your tummy is, however, limited in the ways in which it is able to communicate its displeasure and will be unlikely to write a sharply worded letter to the *Daily Mail*.

Instead it will either inform you directly or it will inform those around you. It will inform you personally by means of a sharp intense tummy ache. This will feel like a small incendiary device going off in your inner regions or a midget trying to hack his way out of your intestines with a scimitar.

Or alternatively your tummy will inform everyone else within earshot about the disgraceful treatment to which you have been subjecting it by making a range of extraordinary noises. It may attempt to inform everyone within noseshot as well by producing a range of extraordinary smells.

The noises emitted by your tummy may include a series of squeaks and rumbles which resound at various levels. These may range from high-pitched tones to extremely deep frequencies.

These could be low enough to set nearby crockery rattling, to worry your neighbours that an earthquake is about to occur, to make passers-by believe that you are in the process of recording some background music for use by the BBC Radiophonic workshop or to cause whales to beach themselves on the shoreline close to your home.

Many of us wrinklies live with persistently gurgling tummies. This presents a dilemma. Should you comment on the gurgle immediately or should you say nothing and pretend it wasn't you?

It is probably best to admit your insides are gurgling if the noise persists to the point where others get up to check the boiler is working properly or to call out an engineer.

If you admit to the gurgling, this may also prove embarrassing. You will then have to keep commenting every time it recurs while attempting to massage your stomach in front of everyone in a desperate effort to stop the noise.

The causes of tummy trouble can include constipation, stress, inflammation of the lymph glands, infections such as gastroenteritis or possibly that extra large helping of pie and mash followed by apple pie and custard you had a couple of hours ago.

Various treatments exist to alleviate the symptoms, including indigestion tablets, medicines and effervescent antacids for the sufferer. In addition, earplugs and a wooden pole with which to open the window may help the sufferer's wrinkly partner.

Alternative traditional treatments for tummy trouble include eating ginger, peppermint or liquorice. Drinking salt water is also said to be effective as is eating burnt toast.

Possibly these cures will not do you much good, but you will at least be distracted by the horrible taste. And clearly, if you are suffering from extreme tummy problems, the best thing will be to jump in the ocean armed with a toaster.

The Wrinkly Guide To Being Very, Very Drunk

As if you needed a guide! The only guide you probably need is one to get you home from the pub after a few too many sherbets. But as with anything there are dos and don'ts involved, and it might be wise to be familiar with them.

Do	Don't
Remember those recommended alcohol units are weekly, not daily	Imagine that if you drink straight from the bottle it counts as only one unit
Enjoy yourself	Do your version of the Dance of the Seven Veils on a table top
Try to keep track of when it's your round	Keep a running total on a pad and produce it when your round's more expensive
Keep up a lively conversation	Have a rant that sounds like a party political broadcast on behalf of the Nazi party
Buy the bar person a drink once in a while	See it as a bribe to stay open past hours
Leave the pub quietly when it's late	Suddenly remember that you are Frank Sinatra/Judy Garland and treat the world to your entire back catalogue
Stay sober enough to get home in one piece	Get so drunk that you have no idea where home is let alone get back there

What with pub drink prices, the concern about dodgy people out on the street after dark (not solely drunk fellow wrinklies, of course), and unreliable public transport, many wrinklies prefer to drink at home.

That makes a lot of sense, but even at home there a few basic rules to follow.

Do	Don't
Make sure you have enough drink in the house to start with and don't have to traipse round convenience stores at midnight	Feel compelled to drink the entire lot before going to bed
Try to have something to nibble on to "soak up the alcohol"	Embark on cooking "a nice curry" after consuming your own body weight in alcohol – the curry may turn out hotter than you think when the kitchen goes up in flames
Invite some friends round to join in the fun	Suggest a game of Strip Rummikub to "liven things up a bit"
Try to be considerate of your neighbours	Think that knocking on their door at midnight and inviting them in will go down very well
Try to be a good host and give your home the ambience of a friendly pub	Keep your spirits in wall-mounted optics and start ringing a bell at 11.00pm on the dot

Things You Eat And Drink
That You Probably Shouldn't

The list is probably as long as your wrinkly arm. Let's be honest, if it tastes nice, it's probably bad for you; if it's fattening, it's almost certainly bad for you; if it makes you feel good, it's definitely a killer. The disgraceful wrinkly response is, of course: Bring it on!

Quite frankly at your time of life, you've had it up to here with being nannied, preached to and patronized. You've read enough health warnings to cover Kilmarnockshire in ten-point type, you've been harangued, bullied, talked down to, hassled, harried and scared half to death. But now the wrinkly worm has turned. You're going to eat and drink what you damn well please and to hell with the consequences.

Biscuits
A cup of tea without a biscuit is like a boat without an ocean, a garden without flowers, Eric without Ernie – unthinkable. Though quite why this gives you the excuse to devour half a packet of the blighters at one sitting is anyone's guess.

Fry-ups
When you were working, a fry-up was an occasional weekend treat, but now the day stretches before you just waiting to be filled with self-indulgence, the fry-up can be brought into service daily. Most wrinklies should probably be fitted with a fryometer on retirement to monitor their cholesterol levels. It's probably already being mooted by some muesli-muncher.

Soup

There's something hearty about a nice bowl of soup, and at your age you need all the hearty you can get. Show us a wrinkly kitchen cupboard and we'll show you a stash of soup large enough to make a Salvation Army officer green with envy.

You may have heard the (probably apocryphal) story of the wrinkly at a three-course dinner ordering soup, soup, and soup – with, presumably, a soupçon of soup on the side. Excuses range from: "I can't chew anything these days" to "It's cheap and nourishing". Well, yes, but does that mean you need an annual intake that could sink the *Ark Royal*?

Alcohol

The wrinkly relationship with the demon booze has been addressed elsewhere in this book, but suffice to say, the more you're enjoying it, the more likely it is you're overdoing it. But what a way to go!

Sweets

It's a funny thing, isn't it, that when you're a kid you love sweets, then as an adult you drift away from the fold a little only to return with your sweet tooth throbbing with anticipation as you approach your dotage? It must be all that hanging around with grandchildren.

And it's not just any old sweet. You rarely see a pensioner with a sherbet fountain or a fistful of spacedust or Toxic Waste. It's either going to be a boiled sweet or a mint. If you ever go on *Mastermind,* this will undoubtedly be one of your specialist subjects. "Ah yes, Mr Humphreys, but I think your researcher might have mistaken the Everton for the Murray mint. Can we stop the clock?"

Tell-Tale Signs That You've Been Overdoing It

Hangover

A hangover is the traditional response you receive from your body following a period (i.e. a lifetime) of overindulgence. That's gratitude for you, isn't it? You show your body a good time and this is how it repays you?

A hangover may comprise a headache, a feeling of nausea and a sensitivity to light and noise. Alternatively these symptoms may just be what reality feels like for any wrinkly if he/she makes the mistake of sobering up a bit. Traditional cures for hangovers include eating raw eggs, pickled sheep's eyeballs or getting blind drunk all over again.

Hangovers are also said to get increasingly worse the older you get. But then the same can be said of many things.

Seeing double

A bit of overindulgence may make you begin seeing double. This is caused by your brain trying to help you enjoy yourself even more than were doing already.

The presence of just one or two other people standing around you will now begin to appear like a decent-sized crowd. Suddenly you will find yourself in the presence of twice the number of friends you previously thought you had and you will be able to have a small party with them.

Alternatively you may be surrounded by twice the number of policemen you previously thought were there. This will also be useful, as it will make it easier for them to get you back up on your feet.

Blurred vision
You know you've been overdoing it if you call out your TV repairman to fix your vertical and horizontal hold and he informs you that you aren't actually watching television at the moment.

Overindulgence may result in blurred vision, but try to remain positive. This may be a good thing if you are surrounded by particularly ugly people at the time.

Face changing colour
Not content with making your own vision go funny, your overindulgence may be so severe that it will begin to distort the vision of those around you. It will do this by making your face change through a series of odd hues, ranging from bright pink to deep purple. Those around you may start checking that their light fittings are working properly or that the lenses of their glasses haven't been accidentally dipped in beetroot juice. Unfortunately the reason is that your face has started operating as a colour-coded indicator of your state of inebriation. If you were driving, the police wouldn't need to use a breathalyzer, just a colour chart.

Heart beating rapidly
This is worrying, particularly if you notice it is being accompanied by your face changing colour (see above) in time to the pounding rhythm coming from your chest. Try sitting down and resting until it settles down a bit.

Heart not beating at all
If it settles down this much, this is quite worrying and you should immediately seek a jump-start from a younger person.

Chapter 10:
How To Find
Disgraceful New Friends

What is a friend? A friend is someone who is always there for you. A friend is someone who takes note of all your worries and concerns. A friend is someone who listens to you whatever old rubbish you happen to be coming out with at the time.

Of course, this could also be the definition of a stalker or a private detective who has bugged your house in an effort to dig up some sensitive information about you.

But a true friend is someone who sticks with you through the years. Through the good times and the bad, they always make the effort to stay in touch. Wherever you go, they will always track you down. Possibly this is because they are waiting for you to pay back that small loan they gave you in 1988.

We wrinklies who are growing old disgracefully may, however, wish to find some new friends. There may be many reasons for this.

Time, the old enemy, may have caused your old friends to have scattered or to have moved far away or even to have been lost.

Or perhaps that's just what your old friends have told you in order to stop you coming round bothering them all the time.

Nevertheless, if you are growing old disgracefully, you will almost certainly make new acquaintances as a result of the excessive, indulgent and possibly physically uncomfortable activities to which you are now devoting your leisure time.

It is possible that your disgraceful pursuits did not appeal to your old wrinkly friends.

Perhaps old Bert from the dominos club didn't fancy joining you for an all-night rave. Possibly Vera from the Women's Institute was unable to find a skin-tight rubber S&M bondage suit in her size. Maybe nude pole dancing wasn't the way the vicar and his wife wished to spend their time.

Or, of course, maybe some of your old wrinkly friends did join you on a disgraceful evening out – and that was what finally finished them off.

So now you have the opportunity to make some exciting new friends.

You might think that young people do not want to be friends with a wrinkly, but this may not be the case. Young people may appreciate hanging out with someone who has a lifetime's (or, as they might see it, several lifetimes') worth of knowledge and experiences to share.

You can regale them with stories of the classic rock festivals you attended in your youth, the exotic places you've visited and the celebrities you've met. OK, you might have to lie profusely if the only such anecdote you have involves bumping into the Nolan Sisters at Blackpool Pleasure Beach.

And then the next time you hold a party at your house, the members of the bowls club, the gardening society and the British Legion can mix with a selection of punk rockers, supermodels and well-built young men with oiled muscles.

Old Wrinkly Friends Compared To New Wrinkly Friends

A lot of your old wrinkly friends were not wrinkly when you first met them. Although they have got older, you can still remember when they did wild, impulsive and youthful things – like using the upstairs toilet instead of the downstairs one.

But with your new wrinkly friends you have never known them any other way. You can't really imagine them ever being young.

To many a younger person, the glass is always half-full. To a wrinkly, the glass is not only half-empty, it's got a flipping chip in it and lipstick smears and something wriggling its legs around in the bottom.

And this is how it is with new wrinkly friends. You will have never known their young, carefree days when they decided to go off on a mad weekend somewhere at the drop of a hat. You will have known them only since even a trip to the post office required almost military planning, what with three layers of clothing, all requisite medical supplies packed and the informing next-of-kin about their movements.

With your old wrinkly friends, you can reminisce about the good old days – e.g. when you could still remember things.

When you look at a new wrinkly friend, you see someone a bit long-in-the-tooth, far older than yourself obviously, because in your mind you are still 45. Similarly, your old wrinkly friends are people you might once have gone to the Glastonbury festival with and cannot therefore be old.

Things Guaranteed To Offend Almost Everyone

It's actually quite difficult to offend everyone. While some people will be offended by swearing on TV, others will complain if the words are bleeped out – probably because they're always keen to learn a few new ones.

While those leaning to the left will be offended by sexist or racist language, those leaning to the right may think that any censorship is "political correctness gone mad" and add in a few colourful phrases to make sure the point is not lost on anyone.

However, certain things are guaranteed to get up everyone's noses.

Being old
Yes, just being old is enough to offend everyone. It offends young people because the wrinkles, liver spots and unplanned facial hair are alien to their unblemished complexions and it offends older people because it reminds them that they look like that too.

Examining handkerchiefs
Why do some people examine their handkerchiefs after blowing their noses? What are they expecting to find – gold dust? Fabergé eggs? The answer to the meaning of life?

Describing your operations
The only good thing about going in for an op is that you can dine out on the story forever afterwards. Though whether people really want a blow-by-blow account of your hernia operation while they're eating their dinner is another matter.

Being The Only Wrinkly In A Gang Of Youths

If you live in some of the rougher areas of our green and pleasant land, you may have found the best way to survive is in a "if you can't beat 'em, join 'em" relationship with the local hoodies. That way you can earn a bit of "respec" whilst not being parted forcibly from your pension money.

Just because your pitbull terrier named "Tyson" is wearing a tartan coat, it doesn't mean to say you cannot become, literally, one of the gang.

It's all about fitting in, but with your own wrinkly twist. For example:

Low-slung jeans

At your age you want to dress for comfort, so having the crotch of your jeans flapping around your thighs is going to be a bit uncomfy. Simply wear normal jeans and have another pair sewn on halfway down to give that "in the hood" look.

Hoodie

It's surprising that more wrinklies don't wear hoodies. They're nice and warm, especially for balding pates; they're cheap and they have those nice deep pockets for storing packets of Werther's Originals, various medications, bus passes, glasses and all the rest of the wrinkly paraphernalia.

Trainers

Many wrinklies have discovered just how damned comfy trainers are compared with shoes. It's almost worth joining a gang of feral youths just to avoid bunions.

Scarf round face

A classic method for young hoodlums to avoid being recognized on CCTV when involved in nefarious activities. Hopefully no one will suspect that you are doing it simply to keep warm.

Graffiti

Street kids like to put their own personal "tag" onto walls – often in places that seem inaccessible and will have therefore involved quite a bit of impressive derring-do to reach. In your case, this may mean putting your tag at eye-level on a wall as anything higher or lower will result in your back giving out.

Vandalism

In your estimation, most of the vandalism in your area has been done by town planners and property developers. Therefore, smashing up some of these architectural monstrosities will not be vandalism at all – more of a public service. At least, that's what you'll be telling the magistrates when you and the gang are pulled in.

Petty crime

These days, you may be quite often walking out of a shop without paying not because you are a shoplifter but because you had completely forgotten to stump up. You will then be non-plussed by the resultant high-fiving and murmurs of "respec" from your fellow gang members.

Drug-taking

Even the most street-hardened hoodie will step back in awe at your frequent pill-popping. Your street cred might be dented somewhat, though, if you reveal that they are aspirins to thin the blood or extra-strong mints.

New Aliases You May Care To Adopt

If you're going to reinvent yourself as a disgraceful wrinkly, you may feel you need a new name to go with your new image. There's not much point in trying to be a cutting-edge codger with a name like Bert Groggins or Daphne Spode. No, you need a new name to go with your new image. How about choosing from one of these:

Usain Boult
It combines the idea of speed (from Usain Bolt) with culture (as in Sir Adrian Boult). Yes, you could say you were a lightning conductor.

Madonna Kebab
It combines a certain outrageousness with a dodgy takeaway. The kind of thing that someone might take home after the pubs have shut but wish they hadn't the next morning.

Lee Van Cleef Richards
Mixing a Western outlaw with a wrinkly rocker, you could get away with all manner of bad behaviour, from holding up banks to holding up against all the odds.

Tarzan Widdecombe
What disgraceful wrinkly wouldn't relish the chance to dance outrageously and inappropriately whilst dressed in a leopardskin loincloth? Ahuhahuhahuh!

Methuselah Laa
You may be as old as the hills, but you're as cuddly, colourful and playful as a Tellytubby. Uh oh!

Beryl Flynn
Just because you're a woman, doesn't mean to say you can't buckle your swash with any man. Splice the mainbrace and prepare to have your timbers shivered!

Ciggy Stardust
Remember when a fag hanging casually from the lips was a sign of a cool and devil-may-care character? Combine that with a futuristic, glam rock outfit and watch your fellow wrinklies go weak at the knees as you sashay into the lunch club.

Concertina Turner
With your legs you may not be able to dance like a rock chick anymore, but you can liven up any party with your squeezebox. Ooh er, missus!

Jams Bond
Producing preserves has hitherto been seen as the exclusive domain of wrinkly women, but now men can join in too, dressed in a dinner suit with a bow tie. The jam, naturally, should be shaken, not stirred, when cooking.

The Wrinkly's Guide To Facebook

Facebook was invented in 2004 by a 20-year-old Harvard student called Mark Zuckerberg. It has since made its creator a fortune of several billion dollars, which has presumably enabled him to pay off his student loan early. Many wrinklies will be disturbed by these facts.

Some will be upset by the idea that this young upstart is earning more during his coffee break than the entire amount of pension they will be given during the rest of their lives.

Some will be enraged at the number of people who waste their time playing around on computers all day.

And several wrinklies will be scratching their heads at the thought of someone who was born in 1984 but who is no longer at school and has got a job (1984, in their minds, still being only a couple of years ago).

Facebook is a social networking site where people can meet and chat. It's a bit like a never-ending coffee morning, but it all happens on the internet. This is the disappointing factor for wrinklies because it means they have to provide their own biscuits.

Joining Facebook is completely free, which should appeal to wrinklies. Some may not, however, be so keen on making lots of private information about themselves available to other Facebook users.

Other wrinklies will be less bothered about this and will happily upload scores of pictures of themselves wandering around naked in their back gardens.

Once you have registered with Facebook, you can start asking people to be friends with you. A Facebook friend is not necessarily the same thing as a real friend, however.

You might not ever meet or speak to some of your Facebook friends in person and they are unlikely to send you presents at Christmas or for your birthday.

Instead of regarding these disembodied people as being active members of your social circle, it might be better to regard collecting Facebook friends as a hobby similar to stamp collecting (i.e. completely useless).

There are said to be almost a billion Facebook users. This means that you can try and collect all one billion Facebook members as your friends. Then you will be able to tell a billion people at length all about the mundane little details of your life and the terrible pain you've been having in your left leg.

It also means that if Facebook were a country it would be one of the three largest in the world. Some wrinklies might hope that the people who own Facebook will now find a country where they can put all their users, as this would leave a bit more space for the rest of us.

Facebook has therefore revolutionized the way in which people communicate with one another. They now don't communicate at all and walk straight into each other because they are too busy looking at little computer screens the whole time-checking what's happening on Facebook.

Places To Go To Meet Outrageous New Friends

Lovely though they may be, the National Trust tearooms may not be the best place to meet outrageous new friends. The same goes for the gardening group and the church fête.

To meet those contrary and individual souls who will add a bit of zest to your life, you must step outside your comfort zone.

Tattoo parlours
Yes, it's true that, these days, you are almost as likely to bump into a Prime Minister's wife as a Hell's Angel, but you are far more likely to meet people who live not just on the edge but possibly under an 'edge too. Try to meet somebody soon, though, otherwise your entire body might be covered in ink before you've got a new circle of friends.

Art galleries
It's strange that unconventional people are so predictable, but go to an exhibition opening of the more outré kind and you will be guaranteed to meet the sort of multicolour-dressed bunch of weirdos that make the Muppets look normal. Just avoid the strong temptation to brand the artworks "a load of old rubbish."

Goth festivals
Now that the Glastonbury festival and others have been hijacked by posh middle-class people in Hunter wellies and designer yurts, you have to stay one step ahead by dressing in black and changing your name to Barzoolian or Xerxes. The downside is it may wreck what's left of your hearing so you won't be able to chat to anyone.

Graceful Versus Disgraceful
New Wrinkly Friends

Graceful: Someone who invites you out for a shopping spree.
Disgraceful: Someone who invites you out for a shoplifting spree.

Graceful: Someone who is happy to share your joys
and sorrows.
Disgraceful: Someone who is happy to share your money.

Graceful: Someone whom you meet regularly for dinner,
a few drinks and conversation.
Disgraceful: Someone whom you meet regularly for a
few drinks, a few more drinks, a few more drinks again
and a few more drinks after that followed by a loud
argument and a fight outside.

Graceful: Someone with whom you can keep fit and
healthy going on long pleasant walks.
Disgraceful: Someone with whom you can keep fit and
healthy running away from the police.

Graceful: Someone who surprises you by turning up in
the evening with a box of chocolates and a bottle of wine.
Disgraceful: Someone who surprises you by turning up in
the evening with a dead body that urgently needs to be
disposed of.

Graceful: Someone who keeps you thinking.
Disgraceful: Someone who keeps you hostage.

Things That Will Tell Others You're Unconventional

It's very easy to become invisible when you're a wrinkly. As you lose interest in fashion, or it loses interest in you and the colour goes out of your hair (if you're lucky enough to still have any) and your face is hidden away behind spectacles and mufflers or sunscreen and sunhats and so on, you become just another member of the wrinkly army.

Did you know there are more than 21 million people aged over 50 in the UK?

How can they be invisible?! Well, there are probably 21 million houses painted in off-white, but you notice only the one that's painted bright pink or in leopard skin print.

So, to stand out from the crowd as a truly disgraceful wrinkly, you have to make a bit of an effort.

Clothes

Beige is banned. So is grey. Have you ever wondered why rock stars wear sunglasses all the time? It's because their clothes are so lairy they have to diffuse the glare a bit. If someone says, 'Do you think you should be wearing that at your age?', you know you've got it right. Think Dolly Parton, think Elton John, and you won't go far wrong.

Home décor

At your age, visitors will expect your home to be tastefully decorated in muted colours, possibly involving Magnolia. What they won't expect is something that looks like there's been an explosion in a paint factory. But it makes it so much easier to redecorate if you can just touch up here and there with any old colour that comes to hand. Think Jackson Pollock, aka "Jack the Dripper".

Choice of music

You might like to listen to Radio 2 because it plays songs from your youth, you might like a bit of Classic FM or even Radio 3, you may like Michael Bublé or one of those girl singers who sings proper songs nicely, but what people won't expect is for you to be "grooving" to some East German noise terrorist band or industrial hardcore. Of course, you can always cheat by not listening to anything and saying it's John Cage's silent piece 4'33'. Street cred without the earache.

Choice of food

The great wrinkly diet has been touched on elsewhere in this tome, but suffice to say it's largely comfort food with not too much nutrition getting in the way to spoil your enjoyment. Invite your wrinkly friends to dinner, though, and serve up something healthy, with small portions and presented like some nouvelle cuisine restaurateur's wildest dream and gain maximum wrinkly rebel points.

Choice of friends

Like, of course, attracts like, so if you will insist on becoming a typical member of the wrinkly army and blending into the background, you will not be short of rather dull company, but if you frequent tattoo parlours, biker-friendly transport cafés, late-night drinking dens, etc, you will meet lots of interesting, and possibly quite scary, people.

Chapter 11:
Career Options For
Disgraceful Wrinklies
(How To Make Money From
Being Old And Outrageous)

Your official working life may now be at, or near, an end, but does that mean you have to hang up your office mug? No, not a bit of it. A whole range of exciting opportunities beckons to the enterprising wrinkly!

What you have to do is capitalize on your strengths. You're old, so that means you have something young people don't have: wrinkles.

Budding artists at life-drawing classes must be bored sick of drawing people with lovely smooth skin and rounded, softly undulating contours. What they want is a challenge! And what could be more challenging than accurately trying to portray the criss-crossing and converging lines etched into that wrinkly fizog? Not to mention the unidentifiable and sometimes surprising hillocks and lowlands of fat and bone?

So, sign up today, you have nothing to lose but your clothes!

If you find the thought of shedding your threads along with your inhibitions a tad uncomfortable, then there are plenty of other opportunities out there for the outrageous wrinkly.

Now that rock stars are getting older and older, you could be a stand-in for one who is perhaps drying out in a Swiss clinic or too comatose to play or perhaps even pushing up daisies.

These days, half the concerts use backing tapes or other tricks of the trade anyway, so having no musical talent whatsoever will not be a barrier to superstardom.

'But won't the crowd notice I'm not one of the original band members?' we hear you cry. Fear not. Half the old bands touring these days don't have all the original members anyway, so the sight of another old wrinkly shuffling onto the stage with them will not be commented upon.

In fact, judging by the age of some of the performers out treading the boards today, it's quite possible you will be one of the younger ones on stage. Rock 'n' roll!

Yes, there are many ways for the outrageous wrinkly to earn a living in their later years.

Becoming a wrinkly card sharp, for instance. You could start off relieving fellow wrinklies of their pension money at cribbage or rummy, then move up through the gambling dens of Soho to take on the world's heavyweight hustlers at Vegas. The fact that they have never learned the rules of rummy or cribbage will be to your distinct advantage.

Or try to set a world record. Something achievable, of course, perhaps the world's slowest ever marathon run.

You could become a model. Ah, you say, but models are young, attractive, slim... all the things I'm not. But that's where you have the advantage.

The next time someone brings out their range of winter woollies, sensible shoes or grey windcheaters, they're not going to want some young air-headed flibbertigibbet modelling them are they? No. Exactly. They'll want someone a bit crusty round the gills.

All that's stopping you is your imagination!

New Jobs For Old Wrinklies

Jobs for wrinklies are few and far between, so perhaps some new jobs need to be created. How about these:

Motorway lollipop ladies (and men)
It's a wonder no one's thought of it before. People on motorways drive ridiculously fast these days, don't they? Hedgehogs, squirrels, deer, badgers, foxes, pensioners – they don't stand a chance. However, with you out there brandishing your lollipop, they will have to stop. Won't they?

Wrinkly footballers
Footballers these days are paid far too much, consequently it's too expensive to get a ticket, effectively keeping wrinklies out of the game. Now if we had a wrinkly league sponsored by ooh, say a surgical appliance company, older people would be able to enjoy a good match at a reasonable cost. The injury time would mean matches probably lasting several hours, so the value for money would be tremendous.

Sit-down comedians
When you see and hear the torrent of filth pouring out of the mouths of some of these so-called comics these days you long for the days of Bernard Matthews, don't you? Or was it Bernard Manning? Anyway, what the world needs is a wrinkly comedian or two to raise the tone a bit.

And why stop there? What about wrinkly chat show hosts, wrinkly reality TV stars...? How about a wrinkly channel? WTV has a certain ring to it, doesn't it?

Wrinkly police

Is that a pension book in your pocket or are you just pleased to see me? Oh yes, the wrinkly crimefighter would have a line in witty repartee that these young coppers just don't have. We've seen a bit of the world, we've been round the block a few times – quite slowly, admittedly – and we know a ne'er-do-well when we see one. Anyone under 40 is a suspect, as is anyone with a tattoo, a shaven head or a hooded top. Pull your half-mast trousers up son, you're nicked!

Eventually there would be a wrinkly TV detective called Inspector Morose or Columbago and the world would be a better place.

Wrinkly soldiers

Have you seen some of the people in armed forces these days? Even half the Captains and Field Marshals look like they haven't started shaving yet. Now, we've got nothing against them; they're doing a good job, but surely a little bit of wrinkly wisdom would be welcome in the ranks? And with wrinklies on both sides, all battles would have at least one break for tea and biscuits.

Wrinkly astronauts

It's one small step for a wrinkly, one giant stair-lift for wrinklykind. Why should youngsters have all the fun? And if they can get a spacecraft to go faster than the speed of light, you'll actually be younger when you come back than you were before you left. Result!

The Advantages Of Offering Employment To A Wrinkly

• A wrinkly will not waste the day at work messing around looking things up on the computer – either he won't know how to or he will have broken the computer as soon as he switched it on in the morning.

• The wrinkly will never take a day off work because he is sick – feeling rotten is completely normal to a wrinkly and he will carry on regardless and come in to work to infect the rest of the staff with whatever germs and diseases he has most recently picked up.

• A wrinkly will never be late for work – all wrinklies are up before 7 every morning and have already cleaned the house and walked their wrinkly dogs before the working day begins.

• A wrinkly will make sure that all younger staff work harder – the younger staff will be sure to keep their heads down all day for fear that the wrinkly will come over and start talking to them.

• A wrinkly will never ask for a pay rise – as long as the heating is on and a tea machine is available, the wrinkly will be happy to turn up for work until kingdom come.

• A wrinkly will have a wealth of employment experience and will always know the best way to do things – the wrinkly will therefore be best placed to stand back and enjoy watching the boss and the rest of the staff cocking up whatever they're trying to do.

The Main Things Wrinklies Will Do During A Day At Work

Switching the computer on
This may take up a surprising amount of a wrinkly's working day as the machine's on/off switch will not quite be where the wrinkly expects it to be. A lot of fumbling around and random pressing of various points on or in the vicinity of the computer will follow. Once the on/off switch has been found, the next problem will be getting the computer to do anything further. This will last until late afternoon when the problem will become finding the elusive on/off switch again to switch the flipping thing off so you can go home.

Toilet breaks
Other people require these every few hours. Wrinklies may require them every few minutes. Most of a wrinkly's working day will therefore be spent traipsing backwards and forwards to the gents or ladies. Ideally a wrinkly should ask their boss if their desk could be moved slightly nearer to the toilets and possibly wedged into one of the cubicles.

Tea breaks
As far as the wrinkly worker is concerned, any time left over between toilet breaks will be taken up by tea breaks. It's obviously a bit of a vicious circle.

Finding your way back to your desk
Well, a lot of these modern workplaces are just unending open-plan offices and the younger employees all look the same these days. Following a toilet break and a visit to the tea machine, some wrinklies may possibly never find their way back to their own desks.

Jobs You're Unlikely To Get But Which You Should Try Anyway

Nightclub bouncer

Nightclub bouncers are normally young, fit blokes who don't stand any nonsense and keep undesirables out of trendy places. You, though, could go one better. The sight of you at the door of some top nightspot should manage to keep everyone from entering the club.

Racing driver

Speed is all relative. While the top speed of a Formula One car might be around 300mph, it looks a little slow compared with say, a space shuttle. If you started an event exclusively aimed at wrinklies, the excitement generated by souped-up mobility scooters taking bends at 12mph would be the stuff of legend.

Ballet dancer

Perfection can be dull, can't it? When did you last see a ballet dancer fall over? You see, you could spice up any production purely by virtue of your unpredictability. The audience would be on the edges of their seats throughout the performance waiting to see if you came a cropper or not.

Tennis professional

Have you ever seen a "veterans" match at Wimbledon? Veterans? Half of them aren't even 50! Let's have some proper veterans out there. If you're still capable of a victory leap over the net at the end of the match, you're disqualified.

Romantic lead in a film

We all need role models, don't we? What's the point in going to see some sloppy romantic film when the leading man and lady look like they might still be playing with Lego between takes? No, we need some leads that wrinklies can relate to. OK, the soft-focus lens might get a bit of extra use, but needs must!

Stuntman/woman

Fair enough, you may not be the ideal body double for Brad Pitt or Angelina Jolie, but if Dame Maggie Smith or Sir Sean Connery need a stand-in, they're hardly going to want some spotty youth, are they?

Computer geek

The problem with computer geeks is that they all know what they're talking about. To really test out a new product, you need someone who's going to say things like "How do you turn it on then?" or "What's this button do again?" Let's face it, if you can understand how to work a new bit of kit, anyone will be able to.

Shampoo model

Tossing your silvery tresses as you scamper through woods pursued by adoring wrinkly men may just open up a whole new target group for shampoo manufacturers.

Pole dancer

Substitute "extra-long walking stick" for "pole" and you could open up job opportunities for wrinklies everywhere.

Jobs Wrinklies Should Definitely Avoid

At a certain time in life, people – all right, wrinklies – are expected to do a certain kind of job.

Waltz into your local charity shop, and you are likely to be served by someone with grey hair. We presume that working in a charity shop doesn't age you prematurely, so conclude that the charity shop is destination numero uno for the discerning wrinkly. Mainly because you don't get paid and what other mug, er, person, would do it?

Therefore, by working at your local Oxfam or whatever, you are marking yourself out as a wrinkly.

Similarly, lollipop ladies and men are not usually sprightly youths, though perhaps they should be if they want to dodge the irate motorists who resent stopping for the poor excuse of letting a dozen children cross the road safely.

Then there are National Trust volunteers. Rock up at Lord So and So's stately gaff that he left to the nation in 1949, and you will invariably be greeted by someone who is a few years past the teenage spots stage. In short, a wrinkly.

How did the voluntary sector ever manage before the baby boomers earned their wrinkles?

So, if you want to avoid being typecast as a kindly old wrinkly instead of the silver-surfing, tattooed rock 'n' roll dude or dudess that you are, be careful where you work. Jobs to which wrinklies may not be ideally suited include those in which attributes such as clear eyesight and a steady hand are essential requirements.

A wrinkly may not achieve great success if, for example, he applies to become a microcircuit assembler, a brain surgeon or even just a simple tattoo artist.

A wrinkly's tattoo work will, for example, be noticeable for being somewhat impressionistic if not extremely fuzzy.

This will not go down well with the person being tattooed, as it will make them look like they are permanently out of focus or vibrating constantly at high speed.

If the selection criteria for a post of employment specifies a keen sense of hearing and a muscular physique, this may again not go in a wrinkly's favour.

The sight of a wrinkly may not inspire confidence if, for example, he is employed as a bodyguard, all-in wrestler, erotic dancer or action movie stunt double. It would be distracting for audiences, if in a new 007 film, James Bond suddenly transformed into a wrinkly old man every time he jumped out of an aeroplane, fell down the side of a mountain or got blown up. On the other hand, the film makers could save quite a bit of money by using wrinklies in such roles.

And wrinklies may also not suit jobs that require extensive computer ability and split-second decision making.

So if you see a wrinkly with his feet up snoring away at an air traffic control desk, trouble may soon lie ahead.

Jobs Only A Disgraceful Wrinkly Could Do

Outrider for Meal-On-Wheels
These days, the meal-on-wheels service has to deliver to some pretty rough areas. What they need is wrinkly motorbike outriders to ensure the safe delivery of their sausage and mash.

It's a good excuse to get the leathers on and fire up the Harley, isn't it?

Roadie to the stars of your youth
Be fair, is your average 60-something gnarled rocker going to want roadies hanging around the stage who look younger than they do? Exactly. Slip on the spandex, turn up your hearing aid and rock 'n' roll!

Tribute act
If you can't be a roadie for one of the stars of your youth, be the next best thing: the star of your youth themselves! Most tribute acts make the mistake of impersonating the younger versions of classic bands. By impersonating them as they are now, you can get away with the grey hair, the no hair, the grizzled beards and the sensible specs and still be a rock star! How bad is that?

Soap opera film extra
Whether it's the Rovers, The Woolpack or the Queen Vic, every soap opera pub has a wrinkly or two in the background to make it look like an authentic, thriving local. Tottering around with a pint of beer or a G&T shouldn't be too taxing for you, should it? No acting required!

Jobs You're Never Too Old For

• Model to appear as the "before" picture in adverts for almost any health or beauty product using a pair of "before" and '"after" images to illustrate their effectiveness;

• Human guinea pig on which Oil of Wrinkly can test their latest products designed to reverse the seven effects of ageing (or in your case the 777 effects of ageing);

• Actor to be seen lying around in the background doing nothing in a TV medical drama;

• Actor to be seen lying around in the foreground doing nothing in adverts for emergency alarm buttons for wrinklies;

• Actor for any adverts featuring walk in baths and stair-lifts;

• Living subject used to portray the dry, cratered surface of the moon during lectures at the local planetarium;

• Living subject on which trainee brass rubbers can practise their skills (without endangering the detail on any genuine ancient monuments in the process);

• Hearing aid tester (note, this job can be prolonged indefinitely if you reply "pardon?" to all questions asked of you regarding the hearing aids which you have been employed to test);

• Object of scientific study (this will also be an option even after your demise – after this, they can study you to work out what killed you; beforehand, they can study you to try to work out how you survived so long).

Chapter 12:
How To Survive
Growing Old Disgracefully

Over the course of this book, we have examined a range of options for those wishing to grow old disgracefully.

We have seen how to dress, eat, drink and smoke disgracefully. We have learnt how to offend as many people in as many different locations as possible. We have found out how to pursue a life in crime and how to spend the evening with questionable associates keeping everyone else in the neighbourhood awake.

Previously there have been very few self-help reference works offering this kind of advice. In fact, a quick check of titles currently available on Amazon reveals that there are virtually no works in print that advocate the benefits of taking up fags, booze and a rock 'n' roll lifestyle in later life.

Well, apart from Keith Richards' autobiography, obviously.

So you may now have come to a decision about whether to grow old disgracefully or gracefully, but whichever option you have opted to pursue, there is one thing that you must always remember: the most important part of the equation is the "growing *old*" bit.

It's no good living so disgracefully that you swiftly bring yourself to a disgraceful end!

It will then be too late to change paths and declare, "I think I've had enough of this life of sordidness and debauchery now. I intend to switch with immediate effect to a life of healthy food and drink, gentle exercise and socializing only with mild-mannered gentlefolk." Furthermore, if your pursuit of the disgraceful has left you fit only for scrappage or recycling, it will be difficult for you to pursue your life of debauchery any further and it will be unreasonable of you to expect others to help you continue your disgraceful lifestyle.

Do not think of asking your wrinkly partner to push you along in your sickbed so you can have another bop at the all-night disco. Do not ask your health workers to ply you with alcohol or full-strength cigarettes. Do not ask the priest who has appeared by your bedside to take you along to a rock 'n' roll show and assist you as you attempt to bounce around in the mosh pit.

On the other hand, it could be even worse. Imagine how you would feel if you discovered you had managed to destroy your health through the pursuit of an overly graceful lifestyle.

Think how sick you'd feel if you had laid yourself low as a result of an addiction to vitamin tablets and healthy exercise.

So instead of growing old disgracefully or gracefully, it may be better to adopt a hybrid, middle of the road, more Lliberal Democrat approach and grow old gracefully with occasional disgraceful interludes.

You could perhaps have disgraceful interludes every other day or just at weekends or if there isn't anything decent to watch on the telly in the evening.

But whatever you do, don't forget to *survive* growing old disgracefully!

Things That You Can Now Get Away With

Luckily, society at large indulges the wrinkly. "Ah well, they can't help it at their age, can they?" "Well, he is 75, you know." "There but for the grace of God…" And so on. This means you have carte blanche to do what the hell you like. The minute your bus pass pops through the letterbox, the sky's the limit!

Stuff that would have been unacceptable in your youth	Stuff you can now get away with
Walking down the street talking to yourself	You are now a "character" (or possibly talking on a hands-free mobile)
Harassing members of the opposite sex	Calling them "darling", "sweetie", etc, and even requesting a cheeky kiss
Falling asleep in company	You can get away with this mainly because half your friends will be dropping off too
Driving dangerously	Dawdling along at 15mph "because it's safer"
Discussing personal things with complete strangers	Detailing your most recent medical procedure to someone on the bus (most off-putting if it's the driver)
Being rude to the vicar	Now you're one of his few regulars he indulges you
Playing on the swings in the park	Just try to remember to take your grandchildren with you

Maxims For Growing
Old Disgracefully

• A little of what you fancy does you good… as long as it's not a vast quantity of class A drugs followed by a short drive at high speed towards a brick wall.

• All work and no play makes Jack a dull boy… on the other hand, you should see what Jack's making in overtime pay.

• Early to bed and early to rise makes a man healthy, wealthy and wise… or, at least, it will make him eligible to apply for a job as a milkman.

• Eat, drink and be merry for tomorrow we die… or maybe today depending on just how much you eat and drink and whether you decide to try to drive home afterwards.

• Good things come to those who wait… as long as they're not travelling on the London Underground at the time.

• He who laughs last, laughs best… or maybe it's just because he's a bit slow to get the joke.

• If life gives you lemons, make lemonade… squeezing, liquidizing, adding sugar and drinking may not work quite so well with other things that life might give you such as a gammy leg, haemorrhoids or a fungal growth on your toe.

• Laughter is the best medicine… although it is disconcerting if this is the response you get from your doctor when he asks you to slip your clothes off.

Celebrity Wrinklies Who Seem (At The Time Of Writing) To Be Indestructible

The Rolling Stones

Ah yes! Surely if you look up the phrase "wrinklies growing old disgracefully" in the dictionary, you will just find a picture of the Rolling Stones. As we all know, the Stones are incredible. They now have a combined age of 273 years. And that's just Mick and Keith.

They have now been rocking 'n' rolling and by all accounts doing several other things as well for over 50 years. This is extremely impressive. Some people are in significantly worse shape having been doing nothing more than a spot of light gardening for 50 years.

What's more, today the Stones remain icons for people who weren't born when they first had a hit single – and possibly not when they last had a hit single, either. And yet when they tour, hundreds of thousands of youngsters will still turn out to rock along with this group of extremely wrinkly old men who (allegedly) have been setting a very bad example for many decades. When people used to say that youngsters should respect their elders, this probably wasn't quite what they meant.

And, of course, at the epicentre of the Stones is:

Keith Richards

A man who is not just the high priest for wrinklies growing old disgracefully, not just their president, their crown prince, their spokesman, their mascot or their poster boy but a walking checklist of exactly what it means to grow old disgracefully.

Keith may appear to some to be a wrinkly, dishevelled, shambolic ruin. Nevertheless he remains completely on top of his game as a legendary guitar hero, genius songwriter, style icon and living (at the time of writing) advert for the apparently reprobate lifestyle.

Of course, Keith's continuing existence might not be seen as helpful for those wishing to promote healthy living. Health officials trying to get you to take regular exercise and eat your five a day must surely curse Keith's continued existence. The people who put warnings on cigarette packets must feel their life's work undone every time Keith appears in public.

Nevertheless Keith still looks like a badly behaved teenager despite the fact that he has not actually been a teenager since the early 1960s. He certainly appears to be a man who decided to start growing old disgracefully at the earliest possible opportunity. Unless of course, he's been having us on all these years and is actually a non-smoking, non-substance abusing, churchgoing, health freak like his older brother, Cliff.

Joan Collins

Of course, in many ways our Joanie is not really disgraceful at all, but something of an inspiration. Born in 1933, but still a sex symbol, married five times, star of the odd saucy film and more than capable of a withering putdown when required, she is something of a role model, or perhaps even a rock 'n' role model for wrinklies who refuse to go gentle into that good night. In fact, as Dylan Thomas goes on to say, "old age should rave and burn..." She's certainly done some of that!

Lemmy

Lemmy from Motörhead is a man who could make certain members of the Stones look like presenters of *Songs of Praise*.

Now in his late 60s he is still touring the world, drinking, smoking, dressed from top to toe in leather and producing a racket so loud that, as he himself put it, "if we move in next door to you, your lawn will die". This clearly demonstrated Lemmy was no ordinary green-fingered, garden-loving wrinkly.

Lemmy's drugs intake has been legendary. After being caught in possession of drugs in 1975, Lemmy had to leave the band of which he was a member. The band in question was Hawkwind, who were not themselves renowned for particularly clean living. That shows you how determined Lemmy was to grow old disgracefully.

If Lemmy were to stop his hell-raising lifestyle, it is believed he would instantly transform into a quiet, meek mannered little wrinkly and/or fall into a deep sleep for the next five decades.

Lemmy thus seems to have little in common with other wrinkly men of his own age – apart, of course, from his interest in Nazi war memorabilia.

He is also renowned for having slept with several thousand women. So clearly that's what women really want. An ageing long-haired wrinkly reprobate covered in moles and Nazi memorabilia. There's hope for us all!

Zsa Zsa Gabor

So good they named her twice! Good old Zsa Zsa makes Joan Collins look an amateur in the marriage stakes. She's been married a whopping nine (count 'em) times. The first time was in 1937 before some of you, dear wrinkly readers, were born. She was putting the va-va-voom in the Zsa Zsa Gabor when young Joanie was but a babe in arms. When asked once how many husbands she had had, she allegedly replied, "You mean other than my own?" Cheeky minx!

Ozzy Osbourne

Bat-biting, dove-chomping rock 'n' roll loon Ozzy has been growing old disgracefully before he was even growing old! In fact, at one point, you may have even got quite good odds on him not growing old at all, but there he is, still going strong, and at the time of writing has just released a new album with his old Black Sabbath mates – and got to Number 1. Lock up your pets, he's back!

Vivienne Westwood

Just her association with the Sex Pistols alone should put Dame Viv quite high on the Disgrace-ometer, but back in the Summer of Hate she was a mere stripling of 36. By the grand old age of 51, she was collecting her OBE from the Queen at Buckingham Palace and apparently forgetting that the dress code may have required knickers. The subsequent press photos ensured that she officially became a disgraceful wrinkly. It may not have increased her chances of a royal warrant, though. We have yet to see "Knickers to the Queen" on her lingerie.

The Disgraceful Wrinkly's Health Concerns – Dos and Don'ts

Do: Eat a balanced diet appropriate for a person of your age.
Don't: Eat a balanced diet appropriate for several people a fraction of your age.

Do: Eat plenty of green leafy vegetables grown on your allotment or in your back garden.
Don't: Smoke plenty of green leafy vegetables grown in the secret cannabis farm up in your loft.

Do: Keep active every day.
Don't: Keep active every day and every night without ever having a break.

Do: Make sure you get eight hours of sleep every night.
Don't: Make sure you get one hour of sleep every eight nights.

Do: Drink no more than the recommended number of units of alcohol per week for a person of your age.
Don't: Get confused and think that "units of alcohol" equates to shelves of alcohol as displayed in your local supermarket.

Do: Make new acquaintances by going out and finding new social situations.
Don't: Make new acquaintances by going out and breaking into their houses.

Do: Retain a positive outlook by looking on the bright side.
Don't: Retain a positive outlook by taking illegal drugs.

Ways In Which Wrinklies Can
Go Out In A Blaze Of Glory

• Overdose on vitamin pills until you literally explode with radiant energy.

• Overdose on cups of tea until you have to go to the toilet so much you completely dehydrate and disintegrate into a mound of dry dust like Dracula.

• Overdose on laxative tablets until you single-handedly cause an earthquake and the ground swallows you up.

• Overdose on Botox until your entire body becomes incapable of movement and you are preserved for all eternity as a statue of yourself. (Remember to make sure you are standing in a suitably dignified pose before doing this so you don't end up preserved for all eternity picking your nose or adjusting your pants, etc).

• Rub yourself all over with Deep Heat Rub until you get so warm you burst into flames.

• Perform a high energy acrobatic routine on *Britain's Got Talent* until you have literally fallen apart on stage live in front of the nation – obviously, if they then put you through to the next round or ask you to perform the routine again in front of the Queen at the Royal Variety Performance, you're in trouble.

• Drive your mobility scooter at top speed toward the edge of a massive gorge and fly out over the edge… or alternatively the mobility scooter hits a small stone, tipping over and launching you over the edge all on your own.

Wrinkly Things To
Always Bear In Mind

• If you think to yourself "I shouldn't be doing this at my age" you are already a disgraceful wrinkly.

• If you wonder what the youth of today are coming to, you are not a disgraceful wrinkly – unless, of course, you think the youth of today are a bit tame.

• If you're always getting stopped by the police, you are a disgraceful wrinkly.

• If you are on first-name terms with all the local police, you are a very disgraceful wrinkly indeed.

• If your other half has disowned you, then you must be doing something right – unless they're the disgraceful one and you're not keeping up to speed.

• If your children/grandchildren are deeply ashamed of you, you're not a disgraceful wrinkly, that's normal!

• If your children/grandchildren are begging all the local care homes to take you as a resident in the future, even better!

• If you are a member of the local bowls team/ bridge club/ keep fit group, you're a lost cause.

• If you are the oldest person in the room at a nightclub/ party/speed-dating event – congrats!

• You won't live forever, but if your life is dull enough it will seem like it.

Things You Should And Shouldn't Worry About

Shouldn't Worry About	Should Worry About
Your hair is turning grey	The rest of your body is turning grey
You fall asleep after a few minutes sitting down in front of the television	You fall asleep after a few minutes sitting in the driver's seat of your car
You go into a room and forget what you came in for	You go into a room and forget your way back out again
Your knees make a clicking sound whenever you stand up	Your knees make a clicking sound whenever they give way beneath you
You have to go to the toilet more often than you used to	You have to go to the toilet before you manage to get to the toilet
Your ears and nose look like they're getting bigger	Your ears and nose look like they're getting bigger because your head is getting smaller
You keep dropping off	Bits of you keep dropping off
You feel the cold more than you used to	You realize you've forgotten to put your clothes on before leaving the house
You suffer excess wind after meals	The Health and Safety Executive have put up signs around your house warning against any naked flames
Your joints ache whenever they move	Your joints no longer ache because they are completely incapable of movement
You forget people's names if you don't see them for a while	You forget people's names if they leave the room to make a cup of tea

Criticisms You Can Safely Ignore

As a disgraceful wrinkly, you are bound to come in for some flak. Younger people will think you're an embarrassment because you are doing and wearing things that are entirely inappropriate for your age.

Older people (if there are any even older than you) will simply think that the younger generation – which, for once, includes you (!) – are a disgrace.

People of your own age will simply be jealous that you are having way too much fun and should be as dull, boring and, not to put too fine a point on it, as wrinkly as they are. Some hope!

So, here is how to deflect some of the criticisms that will come your way:

The Criticism	Your Response
You're dressing like a teenager	I was once a teenager, I'm just getting a lot of wear out of my old clothes
You shouldn't be riding a motorbike at your age	This is a vintage bike and I'm a vintage person – what's the problem?
You should act your age	The whole point of acting is to be someone you're not!
You look ridiculous	Hey, thanks!
You should be setting an example to younger folk, not copying them	What better example is there than not to take wrinklyhood lying down?

Remember, one of the things about being past it is that you're past caring too. And, half the time you're completely oblivious to any of the criticism, anyway.

You don't see people giving you funny looks because you're wearing the latest pair of designer shades or have maybe invested in some of those cutting-edge specs with a little computer screen in them so you can surf the net whilst... well, bumping into things.

You don't hear them making sarky comments because you're plugged into your personal stereo and listening to the latest sounds, or you've got the home stereo turned up to ear-shattering volumes and are break-dancing whilst doing the housework.

If they think you're going to settle down to a typical wrinkly life of pipe and slippers or tea and knitting, they've got another think coming.

You've only just started. That's the great thing about being a disgraceful wrinkly – you can constantly find new ways of being disgraceful.

If they criticize your green-dyed hair, you can change it to canary yellow and turn it into a Mohican; if they don't like your nose-ring, you can put a bolt through your neck like Frankenstein's monster.

And remember, if you're being criticized, you've done something right; if you're being ignored, you've done something wrong.

So You Think You're Growing Old Disgracefully Questionnaire

It can be very difficult for the average wrinkly to assess how they're measuring up in the disgrace stakes. So here is a handy questionnaire for you to judge how you're doing so far.

You walk past the local hoodies on a street corner. Do they:
A. Try to mug you
B. Raise and lower their hands in praise while murmuring "respect" and "we are not worthy"
C. Run for their lives

You keep bottles of spirits for:
A. Special occasions
B. Any occasion you damn well fancy
C. Breakfast

Your idea of dressing outrageously is:
A. Wearing the Donald Duck socks your grandchildren got you for Christmas
B. Wearing a leather biker jacket
C. Wearing nothing at all

A late night for you is:
A. Staying up till the end of the 10 o'clock news
B. Staying up till the pubs turn out
C. Staying up till after all the teenagers have left the nightclub

Your nickname in the local neighbourhood is:
A. The Old Moaner
B. The Boss
C. The Terminator

Your idea of good music is:
A. Chris de Burgh
B. Black Sabbath
C. The shower scene music from *Psycho*

If you see an armed robbery being committed, you:
A. Immediately phone the police
B. Wait for someone else to phone the police
C. Negotiate a cut of the proceeds to buy your silence

When you go for a curry, you eat:
A. A nice mild korma
B. A vindaloo with extra chillies
C. Those scalding hot towels you're supposed to clean your hands with

When you speak your mind, people:
A. Listen respectfully
B. Are slightly worried about what you might do next
C. Cover the ears of any nearby children, then make themselves scarce

Your idea of a late mid-life crisis purchase is:
A. A moped
B. A 500cc motorcycle
C. A sword-swallowing kit

Your home is:
A. A peaceful haven of calm and good taste
B. Slightly unconventional but with a pleasingly Bohemian ambience
C. So manically chaotic that the cast of *Animal House* would be terrified to enter

Most of your friends are:
A. Like-minded wrinklies who are a credit to society
B. Refusing to "go gently into that good night"
C. Inside

When you want to celebrate, you:
A. Splash out on a box of chocolates
B. Splash out on a bottle of Champagne
C. Splash about in a midnight skinny-dip after climbing over the wall of the local open-air swimming pool

The younger members of your family see you as:
A. Someone who blends into the background at family gatherings
B. Someone who is slightly embarrassing at family gatherings
C. Someone who is completely barred from family gatherings

On Halloween, do you:
A. Give children coming to the door a few sweets?
B. Answer the door wearing a horror mask and scare the hell out of them?
C. Threaten them with a blood-stained axe until they hand over the sweets they've already collected?

Every birthday, do you think:
A. I should start acting my age?
B. I should pretend I'm still 25?
C. I'm so drunk I can't remember what day it is, let alone how old I am?

At Christmas, do you:
A. Invite the family over for a traditional dinner with all the trimmings?
B. Invite the family over so they can cook a traditional dinner with all the trimmings for you?
C. Invite yourself to their place, stay for a week and eat and drink them out of house and home?

When you go abroad on holiday, do you:
A. Make an attempt to learn a few words of the native tongue?
B. Just speak louder and expect everyone to understand you?
C. Wear a World War II British army outfit and march around giving orders?

When you get a cold-call salesperson phoning, do you:
A. Politely say you're not interested?
B. Ask them to hold on then go and watch TV for half an hour?
C. Blast an ear-splitting klaxon down the phone?

When you get double-glazing salesmen calling at the door, do you:
A. Politely tell them you're not interested?
B. Display your wide-ranging knowledge of unparliamentary language?
C. Invite them in and hold them hostage for three days?

If the people next door are playing their music too loudly, do you:
A. Go and ask them to turn it down?
B. Turn yours up even louder than theirs?
C. Turn yours up even louder than theirs and go on a fortnight's holiday?

When local election candidates come calling, do you:
A. Say you haven't made your mind up yet?
B. Answer the door wearing a Monster Raving Loony party rosette?
C. Let them ramble on for 20 minutes, agree with everything they say and then ask them who they are again?

When you go out at night, do you:
A. Keep any cash well hidden?
B. Avoid carrying any cash?
C. Keep £5 worth of change in a sock to whack muggers with?

Do you regard other wrinklies as:
A. Compatriots in a world obsessed with youth?
B. Old codgers you have nothing in common with?
C. People ripe for exploitation in your various nefarious schemes?

How do you rate?

Mostly As – As a disgraceful wrinkly, you're a disgrace! You make Sir Cliff Richard look like Ozzy Osbourne

Mostly Bs – You're learning! Keep up the bad work!

Mostly Cs – Frankly, you're beginning to scare even us. Hope we don't end up in the same care home!

Also available from Prion Books

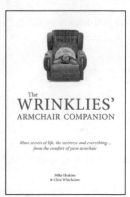

The
WRINKLIES'
ARMCHAIR COMPANION

More secrets of life, the universe and everything…
from the comfort of your armchair

Mike Haskins
& Clive Whichelow

978-1-85375-820-1

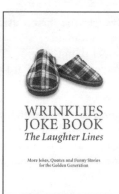

**WRINKLIES
JOKE BOOK**
The Laughter Lines

More Jokes, Quotes and Funny Stories
for the Golden Generation

978-1-85375-657-3

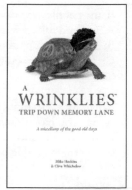

A
WRINKLIES
TRIP DOWN MEMORY LANE

A miscellany of the good old days

Mike Haskins
& Clive Whichelow

978-1-85375-900-0

WRINKLIES
TRAVEL PUZZLES

Brainteasers for globetrotting golden oldies

978-1-85375-851-5

**PUZZLES
for
WRINKLIES**
Clever Conundrums for Older Intellects

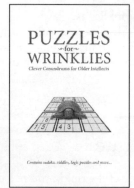

Contains sudoku, riddles, logic puzzles and more…

978-1-85375-775-4

The
WRINKLIES'
BEDSIDE COMPANION

*All you need to know about life,
the wrinkliverse … and everything*

Mike Haskins
& Clive Whichelow

978-1-85375-784-6